OUR STORIES OUR VOICES

BLACK MEN SPEAK THEIR TRUTH | BOOK 1

COMPILED BY JULIA D. SHAW AND TONI COLMAN BROWN

OUR STORIES, OUR VOICES
Black Men Speak Their Truth

Copyright © 2020, The Collaborative Experience LLC.

Published by Collaborative Experience, Inc.
P.O. Box 341377
Jamaica, NY 11434

www.thecollaborativeexperience.com
collaborativeexperience@gmail.com

Library of Congress Control Number: 2020901081

ISBN 9781732840546

Published in the United States

Book cover and Inside Layout:
Karine St-Onge
www.shinyrocketdesign.com

This is the Dwennimmen Adinkra Symbol

It is also known as the "ram's horns"

It is the symbol of humility and strength

ACKNOWLEDGEMENT

A daughter's first love is her dad—and boy, did I love my father. He was everything that a girl could ask for in a dad. He was smart, fun-loving, protective, and a great cook and provider. To say I was a daddy's girl is to state pure facts. Yet, just like he had his great side, he had that other side that could sometimes seem unbearable. But, flaws and all, he was the man of the house. He stayed with us until 2004, which is when he was called home. I miss my dad, and I wish he could be here today to see what his baby girl is up to and the way we are honoring black men with this compilation. After reading these stories, I have come to understand black men a lot better. I honor each of them for being brave enough to open up and share a piece of their lives with us. And I acknowledge their courage, power and strength. Thank you for trusting your stories to us and allowing us to share them with the world. To our co-authors – peace and blessings.

Toni Coleman Brown

Black men go out into the world facing the weight of negative stereotypes on their shoulders, which is very painful to them, their families, and their communities. Many are unsung heroes, like my brother Eddie R. Shaw, Jr. and the Co-Authors of this book. They are ordinary men doing extraordinary things to make a positive difference in the lives of others. Reading and compiling their stories in this book are part of my healing. We love and appreciate you all for sharing your truth.

Julia D. Shaw aka "Julez"

TABLE OF CONTENTS

INTRODUCTION 9

WHEN THE ODDS ARE STACKED AGAINST
YOU – TRUST GOD! 13
   by Kevin Lamar Byrd

TALK ABOUT IT! 21
   by Michael James

WAKE UP! 29
   by Bernard McArthur

BETTER DAYS AHEAD 35
   by Malcolm Boyd

SUCCESS PRINCIPLES 43
   by Jason Murray

THE MAN BEHIND THE THREE-PIECE SUIT 51
   by Richard A. Celestin, Esq.

AN ODE TO AUNT PERZELLA 61
   by Dr. Terry E. Grant

ABUNDANT LIFE AFTER A HEART ATTACK 69
   by Rev. Dr. Phil Craig

STAGE 5 77
   by Milton Shelton Jr.

THE MAKING OF A CHAMPION.........................87
by Phil Andrews

DIVINE CONNECTION...............................95
by Lee Scott Coleman

MY RECIPES FOR LIFE 105
by Shawn D. Farnum

MY LIFE'S JOURNEY TO TRUTH.......................113
by Dr. Samuel Gilmore

FINAL WORDS.....................................123

INTRODUCTION

After the success of our first series, *Delayed But Not Denied, Books 1–3*, we knew we had to continue on this journey. We knew there were more stories like the ones we discovered in our previous books. With this book collection we decided to go in a different direction and focus on the stories of African-American men. In our previous book compilations, the stories were mostly written by women. But, we knew that it was time that our brothers have their say and, boy, did they deliver.

People often say that black men do not talk. They say that they don't open up and that they're often closed. However, just like in our other book series, the co-authors in *Our Stories, Our Voices: Black Men Speak Their Truth* share their trials and tribulations in this journey called life. Our goal with this book is to open a dialog of healing and growth for our Black men, women, and children. Thirteen amazing men of color share stories of love, pain, weakness, and strength. Each has a unique story to tell that has shaped and molded them into the men they are today. We appreciate their willingness to open their hearts—in some cases writing words that they have never spoken to others—sharing a chapter in their lives with us. The book is meant to inspire deeper conversations that release feelings of pain and that will lead to growth and togetherness within our communities. We want black men to share their stories with each other, their mates, and their families and friends, creating new realities of understanding and love for ourselves and others.

As sisters in business, we are driven to help others succeed at their purpose and make their dreams of becoming bestselling authors come true.

Passionately,
Julia D. Shaw and Toni Coleman Brown

✦✦✦✦✦✦✦ ABOUT ✦✦✦✦✦✦✦
Kevin Lamar Byrd

Kevin Byrd is an internationally acclaimed actor, songwriter, performing artist, playwright, producer, and motivational speaker. Kevin has appeared in a number of films alongside noteworthy talents, such as Samuel Jackson and Bernie Mack. He appeared in Al Roker's production *Honor Deferred*, on *Law and Order*, in *Brooklyn Boys*, and was featured in *The Last Dayz*, as well as in the Bollywood film *When Kiran Meets Karen*.

Much to his credit, Kevin has graced the covers of numerous publications including, but not limited to, *AM Newspaper, King Magazine, The Epoch International Times, Vibe Magazine, Essence, Hush, Urban Buzz, Parlé, The Hempstead Times, Blackstar News,* and *Caribbean Life,* as well as *BET,* to name a few.

In his role as President/CEO of the Brown Byrd Foundation, which specializes in cancer outreach and awareness, Kevin Byrd has gained international recognition from world leaders in the form of over 100 proclamations and honors for his prostate cancer initiative. These honors were offered by Her Majesty Queen Elizabeth II, His Holiness Pope Benedict XVI, President Barack Obama, President George Bush, and Speaker of the House Nancy Pelosi, along with some 100 US Government officials, including New York Governor David A. Patterson and California Governor Arnold Schwarzenegger.

Kevin Byrd's upstate hometown of Utica, NY, has designated October 1st as Kevin Byrd Day.

| Email | brownbyrdfoundation@gmail.com |
| Website | www.brownbyrdfoundation.org |

WHEN THE ODDS ARE STACKED AGAINST YOU – TRUST GOD!

by Kevin Lamar Byrd

"Against all odds, when it looked hopeless, Abraham believed the promise and expected God to fulfill it."

–Romans 4:18 (The Passion Translation)

"You won't amount to anything!" he blurted out to me. "I've tried everything possible, but there is just no hope for you. You're reading below grade level, you're falling behind in all subject areas, and your behavior could use some improvement! You want to be an entertainer? Yeah, right! You can't even sing or dance. Just look at you! You don't even have the image to be a star!! You'll never make it past high school—if you even make it that far." He chuckled. "Look at you," he continued. "A couple of years from now, I guarantee that you'll be serving burgers and fries at a fast-food pickup window!"

Influential people have always played an important role in my life, but my father would have never known how his harsh words impressed upon me a passion for the field of entertainment and a drive to save lives, alleviate suffering, and promote human dignity. After hearing his ruthless words, it did not take long before I understood that many of the people that I encountered did not expect much from an African-American boy like me. As a child growing up in Utica, NY, where discrimination against blacks was the norm, I was led to believe that I was somehow genetically predestined for academic inferiority and that all attempts to bring me to intellectual parity were doomed to failure and therefore useless.

I believe that all human beings deserve respect and dignity and should be treated with such. However, as a child growing up, I saw the complete opposite. When I was three years old, my family moved from a small inland town in New York to the big cosmopolitan city of Cornhill, Utica. This was a formative change for my twin sister and me because our parents were dealing with the loss of their first-born son. He had been killed in a car accident. In spite of it all, my parents tried to create memories that were plenty and colorful. I remember sitting by the window and looking with amazement at the congested morning traffic, often cloaked in heavy fog. I recall my first day at my primary school—the friendly schoolmates and the firm, yet welcoming, teachers, and how I learned how to read words out of sheer necessity. I remember coming home from school to a home cooked meal and being tucked in at night. Perhaps most of all, I remember waking up in the middle of the night to the horrid screams of my mother. I would run down the stairs and try to rescue her from the hands of my abusive father. Some nights, he used steel chain nunchucks to viciously attack her. Images of my defenseless mom on the floor being attacked by the man who loved her always made me ponder. Was this love? Eventually, my parents divorced when I was four years old, and my father was given full custody because my mom wasn't stable enough to provide for us financially.

A few months later, my dad introduced us to his new Caucasian girlfriend (who later on became known as simply "mom"). Sooner or later, the horrific cries in the middle of the night began again. This time, though, dad was using his fist. One day, he knocked out a couple of mom's teeth. There was blood everywhere. In spite of the abuse, mom would always come back. By this time, I was about nine years old, and I continued to wonder, "Could this be love?" These experiences gave me a peephole into a sordid world. This is, I believe, where my love story with humanitarian work began. And it's been a never-ending story.

My birth father was a gospel singer and an entertainer, but he struggled with drug addiction and was arrested for drug possession when I was in college. Mom was also incarcerated for drug-related offenses and went away for a very long time. As a way to escape from the stress and sadness of my family life, I focused on ways in which I could beat the odds. I remember sitting in my psychology class one day, and my professor passively stated that "sons of abusive fathers may be more susceptible to alcoholism or drug abuse, criminal activities, thrill-seeking, and violent behavior." She also added that an abusive father can "affect nearly every aspect of a person's life and can lead to feelings of abandonment and inadequacy." I thought to myself, "Daddy issues are far too common in our society."

I know what the research says. Of course, people express these feelings in different ways and some choose isolation, anger, or an obsession with work as ways to cope, but I told myself, "I'm going to rise above it all and not become a statistic."

I have lived a life dedicated to helping others. I began investing in my life's vision at a very early age; however, my first formal experience with humanitarian work started while I was in college. As a first-generation graduate, I was often faced with personal challenges and always had a substantial amount of responsibility on my shoulders. I graduated a year early from high school to escape the terror at home. Although I was accepted into several renowned local universities during my senior year, I found myself declining their generous offers and turning down several full-time scholarships. I wanted to get as far away from Utica as possible.

When I graduated from Long Island University with a degree in the Arts, I was determined to excel, but the journey came with many obstacles and adversities. I was at the pinnacle of my career when I received the devastating news that my biological mom was a cocaine addict and needed help. I dropped everything—my job, my singing and acting career, my car, and my apartment in Park Slope—and flew off to Atlanta to get her into an AA program. She was resistant the entire time, but I never gave up on her. It took a year before she started the recovery process. By that time, I had reached a new low. Suffice to say, I had to work two jobs to stay afloat. One was washing pots and pans and scrubbing floors at a local nursing home. By the time my mom was clean, I had lost everything. I was broke!! I had nothing except for the clothes on my back. In spite of these limitations, I still managed to move back to New York to pursue my dreams of becoming an entertainer. By the end that year, I had reached a financial low, and some nights I didn't know where I would sleep. I was fortunate enough to find a friend who provided me with a place to stay in the Bedford Stuyvesant area in Brooklyn, NY.

In February, 2012, I had reached the lowest point. Life threw me a curve ball, and I became extremely depressed. I had become estranged from my family members, I was working a minimum wage job, I had no friends, and life seemed worthless. I would often go to church to help me cope. One Tuesday night, at a prayer meeting at the Brooklyn Tabernacle, I meet an angel whose name was Karen. I remember that night as if it were yesterday. Karen and I quickly became friends.

One day, when I was down and out, she firmly said to me, "Kevin, you're sitting on a winning lottery ticket. Get up and cash it!!" She was referring to the non-profit organization called the Brown Byrd Foundation that I had started. I had thrown in the towel and had given up hope. But I decided to take Karen's advice, and I cashed in that lottery ticket. Since then, the Brown Byrd Foundation has exceled beyond my expectations.

Karen was a gem and stood by my side when I had absolutely nothing. Her Christian faith showed me what real love was and helped me come to terms with some of the negative things I was dealing with in my life. Karen was a godsend, and she taught me that "God is love." I asked her to be my wife shortly thereafter. Needless to say, my life was forever changed.

The fact that a man's skills can so clearly be predicted by his race, gender, and family economic status is a direct challenge to our democratic ideals. Research claims that a student's success in life is linked to how much money his/her family earns and whether his or her family is well educated. Yet, my parents did not rank high in either category. Through his abuse, my father taught me that life isn't fair. There are no guarantees that we will attain anything, achieve anything, or be loved by anyone. No matter what predispositions we are born with, or what psychological effects may be associated with our childhood experiences, we are the ultimate forgers of our own destinies. I had to believe I could overcome the disadvantages of growing up with an abusive, drug-addicted, and often absent father. I had to believe that I could still determine my future.

I am reminded of a guest speaker who spoke at Convention several years ago. He said that people who achieve great things in life in the face of adversity are living the story of the bumblebee. He explained that this bulky bug is constructed in such a way that, according to the rules of aerodynamic theory, it cannot get off the ground; it simply cannot fly. The problem, of course, is that nobody ever bothered to explain this to the bumblebee. And so, it flies.

As a black man in America, I have discovered that the story of the bumblebee pretty much sums up why so many minority men and women fail. I reflect on how many of my childhood friends dropped out of school, joined gangs, and ended up either behind bars or killed, in some cases. Someone along the way told them that they could not fly. And so, they didn't.

My father said that I would never amount to anything. In retrospect, I could have easily made his words a self-fulfilling prophecy, but something within me prevented that from occurring. I have made it this far thanks to the help of great mentors who looked past the culture, poverty, dysfunction, stereotypes, and skin color of this African-American man. I am grateful for the individuals who saw a follower with a leader trapped inside and gave me the chance to redeem my potential. Indeed, the odds were against me, but my overall experience as a first-generation graduate taught me a lot about myself and made me realize that there are so many other brothers who possess the qualities and the potential to achieve and excel. Every night, I go to sleep overwhelmed with the problematic issues facing the world today, and every morning I wake up and think about what it is I can do improve it. This morning, I woke up and gave God thanks for another opportunity to "fly." I will forever use my wings to spread God's love throughout the nations. I love being a humanitarian because without that, I wouldn't stand where I stand, I wouldn't be who I am, I wouldn't know who I know. I love being a humanitarian because it gives me the tools to envision a world of peace, cooperation, and inclusivity and the opportunity to share those tools and that vision with others.

I am the urban tale that debunks statistics, educational theories, and all naysayers who thought the odds were against me. Everyone will be so disappointed to learn that the man at the fast food pickup window serving burgers and fries is not Kevin L. Byrd. Rather, that man has committed his life to saving lives, alleviating suffering, promoting human dignity, and serving all of God's people—regardless of their economic circumstances, family background, or learning abilities.

◆◆◆◆◆◆ ABOUT ◆◆◆◆◆◆

Michael James

Michael James is a musician, educator, entrepreneur, and proclaimer of the gospel of Jesus Christ. Michael received a degree in Music Education from Augusta State University. With this degree, Michael invested his talents as a Music Educator back into his stomping grounds, the Richmond County Public School System, where he currently provides music education to students in the school district, as well as music lessons to others throughout the area. Michael is also the drummer, keyboardist, youth choir director, usher, Sunday school teacher, ordained minister, and an occasional youth revivalist at Friendly Church of God in Christ (COGIC).

Michael's pastime hobbies are: reading, taking nature walks, listening to and creating music, mentoring young men, playing basketball, dialoguing with respected mentors, and eating. Today, Michael is most excited about pursuing the call of God on his life to teach God's word and to add value to others by way of coaching them toward a spiritually, emotionally, and physically abundant life. It is also Michael's goal to obtain financial independence, with the purpose of teaching others about financial literacy so that, collectively, communities are impacted for the better.

Email	finallythewealthylife@gmail.com
Phone	706.461.3984
Instagram	@twlinternational
Facebook	Michael James

TALK ABOUT IT!

by Michael James

True communication is like an orgasm: without a release, we, as men, can become internally frustrated, maybe even suicidal. The release is not only gratifying, but the release contains the seed to reproduce new life. For mental health reasons, we need to talk.

It was during my time living in Atlanta, Georgia, that I attended a weekly business meeting with local entrepreneurs where the phrase "Talk about it" was birthed. Some of the most "spirited" business meetings with the country's sharpest minds would elaborate on their strategies for success as well as their personal life stories of triumph and tragedy. It was during these 90 minutes of heightened training and suspended listening that I would often shout out, "Talk about it!"

My Pentecostal Church background totally inspired these outbursts! My peers in the room would begin laughing, as we smiled at the awkward timing of these chants. "Talk about it" would become a popular laughing post among my family of entrepreneurs because of its simplicity and insertion into the least expected moments of our conversations. I coined this term during a chapter of my life when I had become silent. I was silent not because I didn't know how to speak. I was silent because I wondered if anyone really cared to hear. Besides, it was relatively easy for me to repress my thoughts. After all, I had been practicing for nearly 30 years by pleasing others.

The art of blending in and accommodating the needs of people had become somewhat of a skill for Michael James. For all I knew, people probably only liked "Michael James" because he was the one person least likely to disagree with them or ruffle their feathers. I often silently wondered if people kept me around only because I was willing to co-sign on all their ideas. Then, I thought, how had this philosophy profited me? Was I better off because I had managed to remain silent about my own true opinions? The hard answer was, No! Then I realized that I had found a new sense of personal expression and freedom when I decided to "Talk about it!" And with this chapter, this is exactly what I am going to do.

Let's talk about my dad, Leroy James. My father is my symbol of manhood— my Superman! Back in the day, he was the man! You heard me!!! Every time I think about my dad, I am still amazed at how my father pastored a church, served as a high school counselor, provided vision for his family, and executed the role of husband, all while being a devout family man. He was always at my games, graduations, and concerts, and he made all my siblings feel the worth of who we were every day. Dad could even make cleaning the yard seem like fun. After raking the leaves and stacking them in piles, my siblings and I would run and jump in them, but Dad didn't mind. He would let us ride with him to the city dump, and on the way back, we would get Christmas morning happy knowing that we were going to stop by the gas station and pick out candy and drinks of our choice.

I watched my superman connect with people in so many ways: as a preacher, educator, community activist, psalmist, etc. To me, he was bigger than life, which is why I wasn't prepared to see him wrestle with his own kryptonite— which happened to be his failing health. No course or class prepared me to deal with this emotionally. Here I was, a walking thesaurus who inspired hundreds on Sunday mornings, and now I was at a loss for words. The man I saw lead leaders now humbly needs family to care for and lead him. Watching my dad navigate his health challenges has been difficult for me. Here I am, now a grown man, and my father seems to be a child. As a kid riding in the back seat of my parents' Cadillac, I remember watching my dad drive us home as I thought, "I can't wait to have my turn to drive." Now, I wish I could get in the back seat again and hand him the wheel.

Every quality I've admired about my dad, I currently see in me. But he doesn't seem present in the moment to assist me or coach me during these times in my life when I've needed him the most. I wish I could cry, but my bank of tears is overdrawn from the many dramatic withdrawals. I sometimes wish I had overdraft protection or some way to get back those things that I've needed from my father to help me take my manhood to the next level—things I've needed to assist me with navigating the pain of being removed from a pool of candidates to succeed my father at the church, as well as the pain that came from dissolving a failed marriage.

When my family noticed the medical condition my dad was facing, we, along with the church family, were faced with a mountain of a challenge. After 32 years of pastoring, my father decided he was going to retire. Neither I nor my church family were ready for this. Dad's retirement from pastoring somehow felt like the "glue" that had been such a healing agent for many in our church family was being peeled off under the heat of reality. No clear-cut succession plan was in place for Dad's transition from pastor. It was mentioned that an election process would occur and that candidates would have the opportunity to cast their vision and be interviewed and voted on. It was asked if any sons of the house were interested in applying. Had this question not been asked, I probably would not have raised my hand. I raised my hand only because, for the past two years, I'd had vivid visions of succeeding my dad in ministry while also experiencing an unusual tug to come back home to Augusta, GA. I personally felt that the events seemed to be aligning to the visions I was having.

Upon entering the applicant process, subconsciously I started to feel honored that I was embarking upon a chance to honor my father's legacy of manhood, fatherhood, and faith. I can't really tell you what that was going to mean to me. I've never pursued pastoring, but throughout my entire life, in some capacity, I've known inwardly that the call to pastor was in me. Senior church leaders and even seasoned senior members confirmed what I felt and sensed inside. To feel that I was getting ready to be interviewed and considered as a candidate was a speechless moment, a moment of awe and gratitude.

But there was this divorce thing that stood over me, like the Scarlet Letter. It was especially difficult when you come from a family where all your siblings are married, have never been divorced, and have beautiful children. The truth is that I had been married for almost seven years to the love of my life. There were parts of those years that were blissful and priceless. Yet there were other times that were just painful. Lack of communication, busy schedules, and lack of intimacy had put a strain on my marriage.

The strain ended up causing a wedge that grew too wide to ever be able to weld together again. I got to the point where I didn't know myself in my marriage anymore. I became angry, heavy, and constantly fighting toxic thoughts. I was embarrassed and felt like a failure. I had to own my shortcomings and recognize that keeping up with an "image" was no longer working for me. I could not fake the funk. Experiencing divorce led to the most painful, horrendous, and terrifying moments of my life. But it had been the right decision for me at that time, and I knew that I still loved God and He still loved me.

Yet God's love was not enough to prevent my name being removed from the ballot to succeed my father as pastor. I felt like my name had been removed from God's grace. I couldn't understand how God's grace was good enough for me to "assist" in ministry—even with my marital problems. I was also good enough to direct the choir—with marital problems. I was fit to play the organ, preside over services, and even preach—with martial problems. But, somehow, I didn't qualify to lead as a pastor. For some reason, my decision to choose "life and mental health" landed me on the wrong side of the gospel, it seemed. I was left with this proverbial question mark lingering over my head: "Can God still use me? Am I a defective product all of a sudden?" If people really knew my heart, wouldn't they see that I didn't aim at ending up a divorcé? I got this way because I wanted to live!!!! Since when did living become an offense that disqualifies people to serve?

Since that incident, I've learned to refocus my energies and eyes on God. My favorite biblical book is Genesis and particularly the first two chapters, where we see a multi-faceted personality named Elohim. He first speaks and then he sees. The unspoken principle disguised in the verses and chapters is that the one who speaks will eventually see. Sometimes, we, as a human family, have failed to perceive ourselves made in the image of a powerful creator with "like" powers to create and give substance to that which is formless. As a result, we don't "TALK ABOUT IT." "IT" represents the unspoken pains, dreams, desires, and hopes that you so desperately long to see come to pass. The proverbial "IT" in your life needs to be discussed so that language can give birth to what's in your womb. If "IT" is a pain you've buried, then talking about it could lead to healing. If "IT" is a dream you're not discussing, then talking about it could help you realize what needs to happen next to obtain that dream.

In December 2014, at an Entrepreneurial Summit, it became clear how silent I had become about my pains, goals, and dreams. To be honest, my goals had been reduced to my roles: paying all my bills each month, maintaining a family, making sure the choir was ready for Sunday morning, and executing my morning/afternoon duties as a teacher. While these tasks were significant and value-adding in their own right, I began to wonder if there was more that my life could become. I came to an awareness about what life could be as I listened to a couple speak that night of ideals that extended past mere survival and roles. It became clear to me that part of what was missing in my life was a sense of meaning that would exist beyond me. As I listened to that couple pour out of their souls that night, I located what seemed to have been lost. There it was, buried underneath mediocrity, mere survival, complacency, and cycles of discontentment and people pleasing. What was it that I found, you may ask? It was my dream. "Talk about it!"

* * * * * * ABOUT * * * * * *
Bernard McArthur

Bernard McArthur is the founder and Chief Executive Director of 3D Inspirations. 3D Inspirations is a corporation that has a focus on helping individuals to develop the right mindset to develop successful practices in order to compete in a global economy. Bernard has spent 30 years in the corporate world observing, analyzing, and researching the secrets of very successful entrepreneurs. He is a former senior vice president, chief operating officer, and chief technology officer, and has Bachelor's and Master's degrees in accounting. He has developed the knowledge and insight to create a methodology that can help anyone transform a stagnant life into a triumphant one. His company works with individuals to prepare them for a productive and meaningful life. They help anyone construct the best version of self to thrive in a dynamic world.

Oftentimes, deciding the next step in a person's career can be a crippling and daunting decision. Some feel like they are stuck at a standstill as they watch others flourish. 3D Inspirations helps individuals effectively navigate the next essential steps to success.

Bernard McArthur is a frequent radio guest on various New York radio stations, such as WBLS, WLIB, and has appeared on several upstate radio programs. He has lectured at major business conferences and at colleges and universities, and he also travels as a photojournalist. He has completed studies on various business philosophies in many countries across five different continents.

Email	info@3dinspirations.net
Twitter	@3_dinspirations
Instagram	#3_dinspirations
Phone	(855) 569-1500
Website	www.3dinspiration.net

WAKE UP!

by Bernard McArthur

After working as a chief technology officer, chief operating officer, and in senior management positions, I watched the job market shift from a position of inclusiveness to exclusiveness. Being intimately intertwined in many computerization projects, I have worked with some of the most talented individuals in the industry. I realized some time ago that advances in technology were fast moving and that the skillset required to stay relevant was ever changing. Therefore, early in my career, I decided to study the impact of not keeping pace with technological trends on a country's overall economic health. And what I discovered is that these major advances in technology have caused major economic shifts in the job market. These shifts are making it increasingly more difficult for the average person to get ahead. We have reached a tipping point, and it's time for folks to wake up and understand the true vulnerabilities that lie ahead.

For the past 15 years, I've traveled to five continents and studied countries that could keep pace with the new market economy and countries that just fell further behind. From the advent of the Internet, to the interconnectivity of global economies, the impact became outwardly apparent when a country did not pass down the distribution of wealth. It's time for people understand that their ability to provide financially for their families and their futures is currently at stake.

We are now in a technological era that some economists have called the Fourth Industrial Revolution. This shift has been so drastic that it is considered one of the most disruptive technological evolutions in the past few decades. With new innovations in technology, there are always winners and losers. Automation and computerization allow for the development of more efficient processes, but these innovations often displace the need for human intervention. More and more systems are being designed to reduce or eliminate human involvement. And with the proliferation of the Internet, there is an apparent increase in collaboration among businesses to move large sectors of our workforce abroad. In some cases, Artificial Intelligence technology not only mimics human thinking but can outperform its capabilities, which further decimates the job market.

A big demand still exists for skilled trade workers, yet our country continues to focus on pushing young people into colleges and universities. These institutions are graduating many students with postgraduate degrees. Some students are even going back to school for multiple degrees. With these types of investments in education, many students are graduating with big loan debts and no jobs. The current student loan debt is in excess of a trillion dollars. Therefore, the return on investment for a college degree is declining rapidly. Getting a good education used to be the pathway to higher paying jobs. Today, many jobs are outsourced and a staggering percentage of recent college graduates are not making a living wage. Job opportunities are shrinking and corporations have discovered that it's more profitable for them to fill positions in countries where the cost of labor is much cheaper. Even with unemployment at its lowest rate in decades, more people are still living paycheck to paycheck. As a result, Millennials, and Generation X, Y, and Z are probably the most highly educated job seekers in the past century. Even when armed with multiple degrees, many still have great difficulty finding jobs in their field of study. Coupled with the burden of hefty student loan debt, many are finding it hard to live outside their parents' homes.

Our economic uncertainty did not happen overnight. It took the collective effort of an entire country. We purchased products from outside our communities. This reduced domestic production of jobs in our local communities. We know the complexities of competing against state-owned companies and monarch governments. We talk about unfair trade practices, but we purchase the goods and services. Our system of free enterprise works when you are competing in that type of environment. When we allow certain trade practices to occur, we need to look within our country for answers to remain competitive. We write the laws and agreements to purchase products and services we cannot do without.

As a country, we have gone from being the leader in global manufacturing jobs to shipping a major work product overseas. We have also moved crucial sectors of the American job market offshore—sectors where we once were the front runners, such as in information technology support, customer service, medical professional support, and financial market support. During past economic booms, America used to be the land of opportunity. Manufacturing jobs were plentiful in the urban areas. Workers could move to the suburbs, where there were multiple opportunities in white collar jobs. A bachelor's degree was your ticket to the American Dream, and a master's degree was a fast track ticket to success. The level of education was reflected in an individual's weekly paycheck. The first, second, and third industrial revolutions provided new markets and opened a host of opportunities, where wealth was distributed based on the level of hard work and effort. But this fourth revolution is different.

We have not properly trained or built our talent pool in the area of skilled trades. Therefore, we currently have the most highly educated pool of displaced workers who are unable to enter the job market upon graduating or to re-enter the market once displaced. We have sat back and idly watched the middle class evaporate before our eyes. The path to economic prosperity and generational wealth has been blurred. And the prognosis is worse for people of color. Forbes and Fortune business magazine printed articles that predict the median income for Blacks and Hispanics will be zero within the next 25 years. This is an alarming trend that effects all cultures. We need to work together to reverse it. We must invest in opportunities for all ethnicities. There is enough wealth in our country for everyone to share in its distribution.

In my 25 years of research of studying the market, I found that the most successful people and countries are the ones that are led by forward thinkers.

In my search across international business philosophies, I discovered proven learning methods that were being used throughout the world, from China and the Middle East to thriving third world countries. I decided to take some of these techniques and incorporate them into my own company.

I started 3D Inspiration Corporation to teach people how to develop skills that are currently in demand so that they can be better prepared to work in meaningful way to lead our country forward. Our company helps people develop and expand new ideas and to build businesses strategies that will lead them to a level of success that was once unimaginable. We explore and address topics, such as why are we continuing to see a decline in the job market? What changes do we need in our education system to make our students more marketable? What partnerships are required for better collaboration between public and private businesses? We also teach proven success processes and skills necessary to compete in a global economy. With us, an individual will learn the attitudes and processes necessary to build a successful life plan. We have partnered with some of the best talent in the industry to help people build a better future. 3D Inspirations teaches people and businesses how to develop the discipline used by some of the most successful businesses in the world.

In the last 30 years, we have uncovered commonalities that exist in most successful businesses. There are similarities in all levels of success. We teach these proven methods in a series of workshops. Many successful entrepreneurs and individuals live by the same methods that we teach. We teach a strategy that uses proven success techniques to move a person's career or business forward. Several businesses have taken the initiative to form partnerships with communities, churches, and organizations, because investing in the American family will pay large dividends in the future. To learn more about what we're doing visit us at www.3dinspirations.net.

✦ ✦ ✦ ✦ ✦ ✦ ABOUT ✦ ✦ ✦ ✦ ✦ ✦
Malcolm Boyd

Malcolm hails from the mile-high city of Denver, Colorado, but he has lived on both coasts more than twice. He loves pretty much anything with an engine and wheels. He is a semi-retired Class A welder/mechanic. When he got tired of working for others, he opened a car repair service in Colorado. The business went well and paid the bills, until he got tired of hiding dirty fingernails every time he was away from the shop.

Until he discovered writing, his favorite thing to do was fix, repair, and tinker with any kind of mechanical gadget. He has built several high-performance motorcycles and has restored classic cars. However, one day he woke up and said, "I'm going to reinvent myself." He took some time off and wrote his first, but not only, published novel, *One Way In, No Way Out*. He started his own publishing company, Three-Legged Elephant, and wrote his first children's book. Since then, he has earned his Screen Actors Guild (SAG) card, and he was honored last year with a nomination at the Softies Short film awards for best supporting actor. Not wanting to wait for the movie studios, he is currently in the process of making his novel into a movie. Be on the lookout for *One Way In, No Way Out*, the movie, coming soon.

Email	MalcoBoyd@gmail.com
Phone	415-405-6619
Instagram	@malcolmboyd533

BETTER DAYS AHEAD

by Malcolm Boyd

"The pain that is learned from repeated mistakes is the fertilizer that feeds a healthy harvest of wisdom."

My name is Malcolm Steven Boyd and I had, up until the not-too-distant past, lived a blessed but cursed life.

How is this possible? you ask. Well, without getting into a long, drawn-out explanation, let me say that I managed to take a fairly blessed life and to do everything in my power to throw it away.

The youngest of five children, I was sheltered throughout my adolescent years. Growing up in Colorado, I never really knew poverty or hard times. It wasn't like we were rich, because we were not. I was just blessed to have a mother that knew how to make pocket change stand up and sing in harmony. And what she did with paper money could pretty much put most financial advisors to shame. But that's another story.

Once I gained maturity, I did what many underachieving, overactive, know-it-all young men do: _NOTHING_. Well, that's not completely true. I did a lot— but nothing worthy of reporting. By my mid-30s, when the rest of my peers had woken up and made career and life adjustments towards a successful future, I was still trying to keep the fun times alive. Some-blessedly-how, I found myself flying high and mighty with a wife and man-child. The only problem: I was still rudderless.

35

I was consistently inconsistent. Despite the many years of trying to do the right thing as father and husband, I still screwed up. Nevertheless, my son still achieved his manhood and has been blessed. He has turned out to be quite a fine young man. He has a lot of my instincts and intuitiveness. Fortunately, he's blessed to get his behavior from his mother. My marriage, however, wasn't as fortunate. I walked away from a wrecked marriage. Thankfully, all players involved are still in one piece, both mentally and physically. For that, I would say I am blessed!

At that time, I was closing out my 40s, and I was "single and ready to mingle." I thought to myself: *Why not start the party again?* And, like most poorly designed plans, it lasted just long enough for me to go fast enough and get far enough off the ground before realizing: "Mission control, we have a problem."

And KA-BOOM! I crashed and burned. My physical and mental health took a small hit—as did some of my societal liberties—but I survived. I guess I have my parents to thank for building me to last, because everything else was wiped out: financially, socially, and spiritually. Once again, I was cursedly blessed, or blessedly cursed—I don't know which one.

Have you ever heard the legend of the phoenix? Not the city in Arizona, but the story of the firebird that rose from the ashes of its past life, a kind of rebirth, or a blessed second chance, if you choose. I believe this is me, because the blessings in my life never stop flowing.

I made up my mind to reinvent myself. First, I had to find something I loved. For me, my *'something'* is writing, so it was natural that I would write a book. I sat down in the month of April with pad and pencil in hand, and by December I had a large enough manuscript to produce three novels. *Okay,* I thought, *this is going to be easy.* I managed to get my work in front of a publisher, who gave me a contract on my first try.

This is when my instincts <u>should</u> have told me, *"If it's too good to be true, then it probably is."* Let's just say that my publisher left a lot to be desired: There were a lot of promises made, none of which were kept. For a first-time author who had pulled himself out of a self-made nightmare only a few years prior, this was enough to start that annoying voice of self-doubt. When I finally woke up and realized I was pretty much on another dead-end road, again I refused to give in, and I went through the storm to get my publishing rights back. I also packed my stuff and got on a plane headed for the East Coast.

Stepping off a Virgin Airlines flight from San Francisco in mid-September, I arrived in New York City just in time for the Brooklyn Book Fair, one of the largest book fairs in the country. This was barely more than four years removed from my previous life's disaster, and only a few months north of the aforementioned publishing kerfuffle—but despite it all, I was better off than expected.

I had no real formulated plan for what I wanted from this great city, other than to get my novel the attention that I felt it deserved. With book in hand and my sister as my compass (she is a transplanted NYC native), I went on the attack. I shook hands and read my book at events and to everyone and anyone that would give me the time of day. I did everything but kiss babies and promise a chicken in every pot. If I had been running for office, I'm sure I would have gotten a fair turnout at the polls. I wish I could report that my novel is currently in the running for a Pulitzer, or has been at the top of The New York Times All-Time Best Sellers List, but I can't.

I sold a fair number of copies and the book received great reviews from such professionals as Leslie Katz, the Arts and Entertainment editor at the San Francisco Examiner Newspaper. The positive response to *One Way In, No Way Out* was very encouraging for me . . . so much so that I published a second novel, *Mann In The Middle*, and I'm about to release my third book, *Bad Day, Good Night*. I was also inspired enough to author a children's book, *My First Train*.

Along the way, I also started my acting career! I am now an official member of the Screen Actors Guild and, as of December 2019, I have started production on the film adaptation of my first novel. I even went so far as to be nominated for 'Best Supporting Actor in a Short Film' at the *2019 Softies Short Film Festival Awards*. I didn't win, but think about this: Less than 10 years ago, I was working as a welder in a small metal shop in Denver, worrying about an upcoming court date because I had made the *repeated* mistake of trying to get rich quick in every wrong way you can imagine.

At that point in my past life, if it could go wrong, it did—and if it didn't go wrong, I would push my luck until it finally did. No one I knew, including myself, believed that anything in my future involved a positive and/or uplifting outcome. Through it all—the dark moments, wrong moves, ill-conceived efforts and downright no-no's—I never stopped believing in myself. Deep down inside, I knew that there were better days left for me.

In 2017, along with my sister's tireless efforts, I started Three-Legged Elephant Publishing Co. Starting a business isn't an easy task, and we have spent many long hours trying to make it fly. As difficult as it has been, it is just like the road I have taken to self-fulfillment. It provided the proof I needed and ended up being the proof I was looking for.

A few years ago, when I started this journey, I took a small step: I wrote a book. Once that was completed, I had to figure out the next step, which, to my surprise, wasn't that hard. The positive energy that I generated by writing the book led me into the next positive thing, which, in turn, put me in the fast lane. I was no longer simply stepping, but *running*, almost effortlessly, to where I am today.

I never considered myself a victim. Honestly, I realized I was victimizing myself. In other words, I kept repeating the same mistake over and over again. One day, I woke up to the fact that my life wasn't on the path I wanted. I knew that it wasn't going to change just because I wanted it to. So, for the first time, I tried something different. I was good at spotting and helping out everyone in my circle—but I wouldn't listen to my own advice. So, I stopped doing that. I became my own life coach. I spoke to myself out loud about what had gone wrong the last time I'd fallen short. I talked about how I wanted my day to go, and how I planned on achieving each task.

This worked! Think about it! Who knows you better than you? No one. Who better to check you on your own B.S. than yourself? Who knows your good and bad sides? You and you alone. So, who's better to coach you than *you*? If you are playing with a full deck and are serious about change, success, and fulfillment, then try it first before you knock it. But don't go running out of the house and talking to yourself to the point people start to avoid you. My method is about making plans and discussing them with yourself (out loud) as you write them down. Have a debate, if that's what it takes to get the answer you like!

I'm not talking about daily affirmations; there's nothing wrong with them, but we need to take it to another level. I'm talking about how I plan on doing a task. What to do and not do, what to watch out for. And I give myself friendly reminders when I find myself going astray, like, *"Remember what happened the last time I got carried away? Now slow down and stay focused, Malcolm."* No. Let me retract that last statement. I rarely use my name when I self-talk, since I am not two people having a discussion.

A spoken word can stop a war, bring tears to the eyes, and convince a group of hostile people to re-think their anger. It can make a celibate person remove their clothes to lie with you. Words have the power to permanently change what physical force can only temporarily hold at bay. So, speak life.

There's a saying that I really like, and it is just as profound as it is short: *"You can't keep it, if you don't give it away."*

For those who don't understand what's being said in those words, it is simply this: *By sharing with others what I have experienced—what works and doesn't work and how I applied that knowledge—helps to keep me sharp, on point, and focused.*

Hence the statement: *You can't keep it, if you don't give it away.*

This journey is in no way complete. I have met and enjoyed each and every person along the way. The good and bad. They have all had a hand in making me become the person that I am today.

I want to say, "Thank you, all," and I hope to meet many more in the **better days ahead.**

✦✦✦✦✦✦ ABOUT ✦✦✦✦✦✦
Jason Murray

Jason Murray is a father, grandfather, entrepreneur, community servant, organizational leader, and author. Raised in the Bronx, NY, by a single parent, Murray achieved scholastic success in school and developed business skills, marketing acumen, and consultative aptitude in the corporate world in a career that spanned three decades. He worked in the consumer goods, publishing, pharmaceutical, healthcare, and financial services industries.

The corporate world gave Jason the ability to foster and develop numerous relationships nationally and instilled in him the importance of business expansion and economic development through challenging experiences and consistent career advancement. Currently a serial entrepreneur, consultant, and thought leader, Murray is charged with providing a blueprint for success. He does this by strengthening communities and narrowing the wealth gap through entrepreneurship education, leadership skills development, and spiritual growth.

Murray is a graduate of Marist College, with a B.S. in Business Administration and a Concentration in Marketing. He additionally holds the Series 7, Series 66, and Life and Health Insurance licenses.

Jason became a widower at an early age; thus, he was a single parent himself for three years. He currently resides in Teaneck, NJ, with his present wife, Tanya. He raised six children through a blended family and has nine grandchildren, which give him a clear understanding of his ever-evolving legacy!

Phone	201-314-8301
Email	abundantnetworkceo@gmail.com
World Financial Group	wfgconnects.com/jasonmurray
Linkedin	linkedin.com/in/jasonmurrayceo/
Instagram	instagram.com/jasonmurrayceo/
Facebook	facebook.com/jasonmurrayceo
Twitter	twitter.com/JasonMurrayCEO

SUCCESS PRINCIPLES
by Jason Murray

I was introduced to volunteering and mentoring at an early age. I'm thankful because it enabled me to realize the importance of thinking of others and not being an individual who focuses only on himself. As a college student at Marist College in Poughkeepsie, NY, I watched how my brother, Bakari Desmond Murray, was very involved in campus activities at his college, SUNY New Paltz. This encouraged me to get involved in my own campus activities. I became a leader in the Black Student Union organization, served as a tutor with the Upward Bound Program, and attended various lecture series at my college. Participating in these activities raised my level of consciousness. My service on campus also generated a level of influence for me. It provided me with the confidence to be a good student and to develop leadership skills rather than acting merely as a follower.

I was able to put my leadership skills into action early in my college years. I can recall, during my freshman year, taking a course in Marketing Management. When I attended the class, my professor, Dr. Lester Cone, asked me why I was enrolled in the course as a freshman when it was a junior level course. My reply was, "It was a requirement and I selected it based on it being a requirement." He said, "Okay."

Most students would take this course after they had completed other prerequisite courses. However, I was confident I could do well and was determined to do so. I ended up getting a B in the course, and that encouraged me to focus on Sales and Marketing as a career. That career has now spanned over thirty years.

Little did I know at the time, but my confidence and leadership skills had kicked into action, and rather than having a limited belief in myself, I focused on a positive approach. That attitude enabled me to succeed not only in that class but throughout my career, despite whatever challenges I might have faced. I discovered relatively early that when you look at matters with a positive attitude, your outcomes will usually turn out positive. Conversely, having a pessimistic mindset is detrimental to yourself, as well as to the people you interact with.

Once I had graduated from college, it was time for me to start my career. I was charged with taking care of my family and figuring out how to assimilate into a society that has not always been fair toward African-Americans in general, but had been particularly unfair to African-American men. This is one of the reasons why I have always been proactive about being the best that I can be in most areas of my life. Because I was fortunate to have mentors, I understood the importance of personal development as a way of keeping me grounded. I would not allow circumstances to control my thoughts or activities, despite unfair policies, racism, and other challenges that can occur as a part of life.

One of the first challenges I faced was landing a job that would provide me with adequate income to support my family of four. By the time I graduated college, I was already married and the father of two sons. While having a degree gave me the basic credentials necessary for the position I was seeking, I was told that I didn't have the necessary sales experience to qualify for a position as a financial advisor. I found this disturbing because some of my peers of different ethnicities, who had sought the same role, had been given the opportunity to prove that they could learn the position despite not having the required experience. While this wasn't fair to me at all, I allowed my leadership and personal development skills to kick in, and I took the necessary steps to get the selling skills required to qualify for the position.

My determination to succeed in the sales profession encouraged me to learn as much as possible about the industry so that I could be as competitive as possible within each role I obtained throughout my career. I knew that, as an African American sales professional, I needed to be a step above the competition in order to excel and grow. With this being the case, I took the initiative to join a professional networking organization specifically for African Americans, called the National Sales Network (NSN). Not only did I join the organization, I also took the initiative to become a leader in our local chapter. For many years, I volunteered my time, perfected my craft, developed leadership skills, and excelled in my platform skills as a public speaker. These activities proved to be very valuable to me and allowed me to receive job offers from corporate partners that had relationships with NSN.

One of the best job offers I received through my association with NSN was when I was recruited by Merrill Lynch in 2006 as a financial advisor. Finally, my dream job of becoming an advisor was fulfilled. Unfortunately, my role at Merrill Lynch was short-lived due to the global financial crisis in 2008 that led to massive layoffs and the near collapse of our entire economy. Fortunately, by this time, I had garnered extensive skills, along with an enormous network. This allowed me to reinvent myself and transition into the Medicare industry, and I was able to continue living my life, taking care of my family, and maintaining my mortgage. Other individuals weren't as fortunate during that period, as we saw many foreclosures and people out of work for extended periods of time. Many individuals also lost hope due to the devastation caused by the global financial crisis. After rebounding from that experience, I was able to return to build my current financial service business as an advisor with Transamerica Financial Advisors.

I'm still active as a member of NSN, although now I serve in more of a mentor role. I mentor new college graduates and sales professionals with less tenure in the industry than mine. I also took the initiative to join another organization, the Association of African American Financial Advisors (AAAA), to volunteer my time and, at the same time, to work on developing my craft as an entrepreneur. AAAA was created to address the needs and concerns of African American Financial Professionals. This organization works in alliance with academic leaders at HBCUs that support financial planning degree programs, legislative and regulatory bodies, financial services firms, and consumer interest organizations. AAAA fosters the value of financial planning and advances the financial planning profession. Since becoming a member of this organization, I've been able to network within the financial services industry with other financial service professionals. I have also gained additional insights into the industry, specifically related to the growth and high demand for financial services entrepreneurs.

My biggest accomplishments and the greatest satisfaction I've achieved while being a member of both NSN and AAAA have involved my ability to serve as a positive role model to young professionals in both the sales and financial services industries. I was mentored throughout my career, and all my mentors instilled in me the importance of mentoring others who come behind me, thereby keeping the cycle of mentorship as an ongoing and valuable benefit for African American professionals. I feel it's my duty to pave the way for others, just as the path was paved for me. The value of my time is very important; therefore, when I take the time to volunteer, provide service, or mentor others, I want to know that my time and sharing of insights is appreciated. Therefore, I also instill in the individuals I mentor the importance of giving back in turn to others by providing the ability for succession planning within the leadership of these non-profit organizations.

I also learned through my experiences that strong leadership and personal development skills are nothing without having a strong spiritual foundation. When your spiritual foundation is intact, you are able to gather strength and insights from your belief system and spiritual leaders and equip yourself with the knowledge that keeping your faith intact will allow you to weather storms and adversity. I didn't always realize the power of my spiritual foundation until my wife, Rhonda Fishburne Murray, was diagnosed with lymphoma after delivering my second son, Jabari. I had to process what this news was going to mean to our family and determine how to best handle the situation. I had to lean on my faith to understand how I would handle the additional responsibilities in my life. I was certainly in unchartered territory at that time, being a student in college while simultaneously working to support my family. Being faced with a life-changing diagnosis gave me a different perspective on my future.

My wife's physicians were baffled that someone her age had developed this type of cancer, when most cases with this diagnosis were seen in patients much older than Rhonda. As we went about our lives searching for answers, raising our children, and praying that she would be cured, my faith and belief were certainly challenged. Thankfully, through all the uncertainty, I was able to rely on my spiritual foundation to help me to take on my additional responsibilities as a husband, father, caregiver, and businessman. Unfortunately, my first marriage lasted only seven years, as Rhonda passed in 1988 after a long battle with her illness.

Now faced with raising two sons on my own, again I had to tap into my spiritual foundation to handle the responsibilities of rearing my children as a single parent. Fortunately, I was again able to weather the storm, move on with my life, and provide for my family. I was able to succeed as a single parent because I knew how to cook, clean, and manage my time effectively, in addition to having a support system in place from my extended family and friends in my neighborhood. After three years as a single parent, I was able to establish a relationship with someone I knew from high school who was also a single parent and raising her children alone as a result of divorce. This relationship, which began in 1991, is still intact, as we've been together for 28 years and married for 25 years. My wife, Tanya Moore-Murray, and I have raised our blended family of six children and nine grandchildren. We've been tested in many ways, as you can imagine, since the rearing of children doesn't come without problems, stress, and struggles. Through it all, though, we have kept our faith and belief system intact and are blessed to have raised all our children, who now live on their own and have their own families. We are following careers and own a successful business.

Another example of my belief system and the faith I possess through my spiritual foundation is my passion and desire to succeed as an entrepreneur. When an individual is talented, has marketable skills, and develops a successful track record during their career, recruiters are always looking to provide an opportunity for this type of individual. When faced with the decision whether to go back to a corporate job or fulfill my goal of entrepreneurship, I chose the latter. Entrepreneurial endeavors can be rewarding, but at the same time very challenging, when endeavoring to get a business to a point where it is profitable and sustainable. Despite the challenges, the rewards of making an impact, developing solutions to problems, and providing a viable service that can benefit the masses far outweighed the obstacles I had to overcome as I became a successful entrepreneur.

As a black man in our society, I'm proud to have achieved success in raising my family while simultaneously developing a strong career and then transitioning to become an entrepreneur that gives me the ability to grow unlimited wealth to pass down to my next generation. I believe that we, as African American men with our God given talents and sense of purpose, can show this society that we represent images that our families can be proud of and that businesses can be developed that our children will want to emulate. Volunteering my time and providing service through the years with non-profit organizations, at my church and within my community, have provided me with an understanding that when one gives, one ultimately receives.

It's important to note, though, that one shouldn't give to receive. Instead, give out of the goodness of your heart and desire to make a difference through giving. I'm thankful that my various positions as a leader gave me the opportunity to develop leadership skills in others, and I look forward to being a mentor. I'm always open to paving the way for others, and I continue to share my messages on leadership and mentorship, along with personal and financial success experiences and strategies, at conferences, colleges, churches, youth groups, non-profit organizations, and corporations. I am available to give presentations on a variety of topics and can be reached at www.contactme.com. I will always be grateful for the foundation I've been given to lead and provide for my family and to create and grow a business, while serving within my community.

✦✦✦✦✦✦ ABOUT ✦✦✦✦✦✦
Richard A. Celestin, Esq.

Richard Anthony Celestin, Esq., is a Jamaica, Queens native who serves as an attorney, an author, an adjunct professor, and an entrepreneur. For most of his life, he has directed his work toward underrepresented and at-risk youth via the not-for-profit sector and with alternative-to-detention programs in Manhattan, Brooklyn, and Queens. He created Richard Celestin Consulting Group, LLC, for the purposes of providing legal skills development, self-awareness, youth empowerment, and consequential thinking programs for elementary, middle, and high school students in the NYC area, particularly for youth of color. Richard also serves as a consultant for various organizations seeking to develop youth-based programs within the community, and he supports others as a success and empowerment coach and motivational speaker, focusing on empowering youth, young adults, and professionals. His self-published book, *The Hard Facts About Soft Skills*, offers insight into the most relevant soft skills necessary to be successful in the academic and professional world.

Email	RCelestinLLC@gmail.com
Phone	(917) 226-0184
Instagram	the_inspirational_lawyer
Linkedin	linkedin.com/in/Richard-celestin
Website	www.RichardCelestinLLC.com
	www.TheInspirationalLawyer.com
	www.TheHardFactsAboutSoftSkills.com

THE MAN BEHIND THE THREE-PIECE SUIT

by Richard A. Celestin, Esq.

A business suit has long represented a symbol of authority, professionalism, and success. The level of purpose and confidence exuded by individuals I used to see in suits as a child, particularly men of color, was nothing short of amazing. As an adult, I take great pride in my professional look, especially my suits. However, I now have a new understanding of the role that a suit symbolizes, at least as it pertains to my life.

My suit essentially served as a mask. It was a disguise intended to create positive and empowering assumptions about me and my success. Don't get me wrong—a majority of those assumptions, as they relate to my accomplishments, have been correct. However, many of those assumptions did not take into account my incredibly difficult and challenging journey before, and the suit became a staple of my professional brand. They did not consider my past failures and insecurities or my ongoing struggles. The finished product would look amazing, but the process of creating that product was anything but.

There is no shame or regret in the process and in my story. In fact, I am thankful for every situation that caused me great pain or had me question my value as a man. I believe, in my heart, that every instance that almost broke me was designed to strengthen me. I didn't understand it at the time

51

but, in hindsight, I get it now. Rather than hide my process out of shame or embarrassment, I now want to share it. I want to shatter those assumptions one may have when they see me in a suit and assume my life has been a domino effect of one success after another, with little to no struggle or problems. Because while there is much to learn from my successes, the real gems can be found behind the suit. What cannot be seen when I am in my sharp and tailored suits can be found in the layers underneath. This is where the three core components of my existence—mental, physical and emotional—have been consistently consumed by pain, challenges, and struggles.

Mentally

Throughout my childhood, I endured severe bullying, both physically and verbally. I was a target because of my weight, my height, my glasses, and my poor fashion sense. My parents had neither the desire nor the ability to spend money on name-brand clothing, so the bullying continued for years before eventually fading away as I changed physically and the maturity level of my peers changed. I assumed that as I got older, this chapter in my life would be over and would represent a cautionary tale that I would tell to young people. However, I would not come to truly understand the effects it would have on me as an adult and professional until later in life.

I struggled with my self-worth or value as a man and as a professional. I also craved external validation and praise to feel worthy and important. Compliments, whether on my work or my appearance, were characterized in my mind as empty attempts to soften me up in preparation for a favor, rather than containing any truth. Any awards and recognitions that I received as a professional were quickly dismissed as being a fluke, because I felt unworthy of merit and believed that others were more successful and deserving than I was. And I developed an innate ability to encourage, motivate, and support others but could not do the same for myself. Wearing a suit was a much-needed disguise from the mental war that was going on in my head, but I realized that the suit was not enough and that I needed to work through these insecurities internally.

Although considered taboo in the black community, I realized that I was not going to identify and work through my mental obstacles and roadblocks without the support of a therapist. Through therapy, I was able to get to the core of why I had such little belief in myself and my abilities, along with why I often engaged in behavior that was self-sabotaging and hurtful to others. While this was incredibly difficult, it was necessary, as I needed to find where my voids were and to explore ways to fill those voids without relying on other people or outside influences. The remedy for many of the battles I faced regarding my value was a relatively simple, but daunting, task. Learning how to love myself and to accept that a man of color in a suit is just as worthy as his peers was no small feat.

So, how does one go about loving oneself? After continued therapy, as well as research on the topic and a better understanding of the voids I was seeking to fill, I came up with three essential practices I needed to implement consistently. First, I needed to believe in and embrace my value and self-worth. This involved analyzing my accomplishments as a professional and as a man and understanding that I was, by any measure or definition, a success. I needed to learn to accept the compliments and kind words, as well as the awards and recognitions, as an indication of my success rather than being a mistake or a fluke. Once I had a better understanding of my value, my next step was to hold others accountable for appreciating it. My tolerance level for any lack of appreciation or disrespect was drastically reduced in any circumstance where I believed, at my core, that I deserved better.

Second, I needed to address my need to seek validation and recognition from others in order to feel a sense of worth. To fill this void, I had to turn down the volume from the outside world and focus on increasing the volume internally. I needed to provide my own voice of praise and acknowledgment, rather than seeking or waiting for it from someone else. I had to confidently remind myself regularly that I am amazing, awesome, and important without any feelings of conceit or arrogance. The volume internally needed to drown out any negativity or doubt cast on me by other people, as well as to ensure that I never had a moment of doubt as to who I was or what I was bringing to the table.

Lastly, and arguably the most fun aspect, was that I needed to learn how to celebrate my accomplishments and reward myself for my hard work and sacrifice. Celebrations took many forms. They were as simple as a pat on the back to a celebratory song and dance in private. I did whatever it took to get addicted to the endorphins associated with accomplishing a task. In cases where the accomplishment was deserving of more, I would reward myself by purchasing something I really wanted or treating myself to a day of relaxation with no work. Rewarding myself was a necessary feel-good act that worked wonders in continuing to build my self-esteem and self-worth.

Today, I continue these practices, although I would be lying if I said that I didn't slip up from time to time. However, my self-worth is strengthened as a result of this consistent practice and has served as a guiding force behind my desire to continue to grow and improve on all levels.

Physically

It is often said that pain, and the process of enduring it, leads to growth and strength. Arguably, one of the most identified quotes as it relates to this concept is "no pain, no gain." However, this conversion of pain into some type of empowering and positive force to move forward is one that is incredibly difficult, mainly because my life has been constantly presented with opportunities to endure and to push through physical pain and suffering and to discover ways to grow despite it.

My childhood, while challenging, was also incredibly fun. I came from a very loving and supportive home, and although we were not wealthy by any means, we found ways to enjoy and appreciate what we had and what we were able to do. Aside from the occasional cold or bumps and bruises, I was a relatively healthy little kid (arguably too healthy, as I refused to give up the baby fat). When high school hit, I underwent a lot of physical changes that began to make me less of a target for bullying and more of an average hormonal high school boy. Life was doing pretty good for me up until my junior year, which is when it all began. I was plagued with chronic stomach pains that went undiagnosed, despite seeing a litany of medical professionals and undergoing countless examinations. My family and I were all confused because doctors could not determine what was wrong with me or how to address it. Junior year came and went with no changes. Then the fun began.

One afternoon, while relaxing at home with my family, I was hit with that same nagging chronic pain. I prepared mentally to deal with it until it subsided. However, this time it never did. Instead, it got increasingly worse. The next thing I knew, my brother was carrying me to the car as my family prepared to rush me to the emergency room. The doctors did not know where to begin or what to do, so I underwent more testing. A sonogram revealed that my appendix was inflamed and was about to explode. I was rushed into surgery, but unfortunately for me, my appendix exploded as it was being removed. Despite this potentially fatal incident, I survived surgery and was then coined "the boy wonder" by the medical staff. Little did they know, but this was a nickname my mother used to call me previously for enduring so much and pushing forward. I was thankful for surviving the ordeal and ready to move forward to recovery and welcome an end to the pain. But pain was not done with me yet.

The complications of the appendix exploding led to infections and more surgeries, followed by a diagnosis of Crohn's Disease, all while a senior in high school. I would be lying if I didn't admit that I considered suicide, believing that both my family and I could not handle any more. My senior year included six surgeries and multiple near-death experiences, but I survived. My final surgery took place shortly after my high school graduation. And while I have been fortunate enough to avoid any additional surgeries, I am essentially on medication for life and have a laundry list of food restrictions, which, if not followed properly, would lead to excruciating pain and potentially hospitalization (as has happened on several occasions over the years).

Up until a few years ago, this entire ordeal was a well-kept secret between only my closest friends and family members. I was instructed, at great length, by my mother to avoid sharing my history for fear that I would be judged or ridiculed for it. So, I kept this a secret, even at times when it was the most challenging thing I had to do. There were times where I would be in meetings and at events, most times all decked out in my sharpest suit, and in indescribable pain, but no one knew otherwise. It was one comment from a high school student during a workshop that shifted my thinking and motivated me to be more open and honest about my pain. The high schooler looked at me in my stylish suit and said that I didn't look like a suffered a day in my life. It was challenging to hold back nervous laughter, but instead I shared my story. And I've never stopped sharing my story since.

In sharing my personal story of how I was able to push through the pain and move forward, I began empowering others on how to do the same. It would have been incredibly easy for me to use my experience to justify any of my failures or use it as the reason why I could not see a goal through to its completion. And I highly doubt most people would blame me. However, I felt the greater message was not that I didn't accomplish a goal because of the pain, but instead that I accomplished the goal in spite of it. Even though I missed weeks of high school while being hospitalized, I still graduated. Despite never knowing when I would have a good day or be paralyzed in pain, I pushed forward and graduated college. Despite staring at my scars every morning, knowing I could never live a "normal" life, I pushed through and graduated law school. Excuses were rarely an acceptable option, because they would pale in comparison to what I had already overcome. I always knew that regrets and failures as a result of quitting would outlast any pain. One of the many lessons I have learned in embracing pain is the absolute need to build resilience. Pain is not a curse but is instead a blessing. I am thankful for the pain.

Emotionally

Depression is not a term to be thrown around loosely, nor are the numerous emotional effects that it can have on a person. A challenging aspect of being in a state of depression is that sometimes we are not even aware that we are in that position. We can sometimes dismiss this feeling as having a bad day (or week or more) or just being in a bad mood for an inexplicable reason. I personally realized that I was in a state of depression when a bad day turned into a bad week and then magnified into what I considered a horrible state of life. However, that depression birthed the most amazing miracle I could ask for.

Upon entering law school, my game plan was to find a way to marry my two passions—education and the law. Once I graduated, my first job was at an amazing organization that focused heavily on education. This felt rewarding on many levels, but it also left me feeling unfulfilled on the legal side and caused me to have an apathetic approach to my work, which left me unhappy and bored. Two years later, I decided it was time to focus on my love of the law, and I transitioned into a role that concentrated heavily on working with justice-involved youth. Unfortunately, I was left feeling once again like I had a void in one aspect of my passion. While I was successful in both positions, I was consistently left feeling like I was unhappy and in need of a change. I essentially felt like I was just holding my breath from the hours of 9am to 5pm. Then, one day, it all hit me like a ton of bricks.

It was a Monday, and I was not in the mood to accept the fact that I had to sacrifice eight hours of my day, but I managed to survive. Once I made it home, I cooked up a bowl of pasta and sat on the couch to watch some nonsense on cable. I ate myself into a food coma. While sitting there staring at the television, the feelings of sadness, being unfilled, and uselessness all weighed on my chest and made it hard for me to breathe. It was at this time that I knew I was not simply having a string of bad days and months or was unhappy in the moment. I was dealing with depression. Suddenly, as if being struck by lightning, a series of questions began echoing in my head, almost if by design. *Is this it? Is this how you take advantage of surviving a medical condition that would have killed most people? Is this what you went to law school for? Is this all you got?* These questions struck me with stinging pain. I felt like I was being hit by bullets. It was in that moment that I decided that I had enough and things had to change.

I made several life-changing decisions that night. First, I decided that I never wanted to feel that sense of depression and being unfulfilled ever again. Second, I decided that I was no longer going to waste time or wait for life to happen to me, especially when I knew that I had the power, intelligence, and drive to create the universe that would leave me feeling fulfilled. But in order to do this, I needed to take control of my life and work on what it looked like—which is exactly what I did. Within a month of that night, I had created a plan to develop my own educational consulting business. Within two months of that night, I had submitted my two-week notice and took some time off to re-discover my passions. As a result of this, I started probably the most meaningful position I have had to date as an employee and created a situation where I was able to appease my desire for education and working with youth, along with my passion for working within the legal field.

Part of my decision to change my mental and emotional state involved a complete overhaul of my professional clothing. The random suits I had been wearing would often fit baggy, with shirts fitting loosely and made of poor quality. This certainly did not help me with my struggles with worthiness. Realizing that the investment was way more than financial, I began shopping for designer suits that fit better and were significantly more stylish. I wanted it to be impossible to feel like anything short of a powerhouse when the suit was on. My passion for suits morphed into a passion also for shirts, watches, socks, and dress shoes. Suddenly, my new look matched with my new mentality and became a driving force behind a great deal of my success.

Today, I no longer need the suit to feel like a success. And while I am thankful for what it represents and how it makes me feel, the suit no longer makes this man. I make the suit.

✦ ✦ ✦ ✦ ✦ ✦ ✦ ABOUT ✦ ✦ ✦ ✦ ✦ ✦ ✦

Dr. Terry E. Grant

Dr. Terry Grant has over 30 years of experience as a Cosmetic, General, and Geriatric Dentist. He was awarded a "Diploma in Geriatric Dentistry" by the American Board of Special Care Dentistry and The American Society for Geriatric Dentistry. He had served as a Chief Geriatric Dentist at major New York City and Long Island Hospitals, Medical Centers, Nursing Homes, and Assisted Living Facilities. He also served as a Clinical Assistant Professor at the New York University College of Dentistry and as a Geriatric Dentistry Expert in 1994 for the U.S. Government Department of Health and Human Services, working to accommodate President Clinton's Health Care Reform. He served on the American Dental Association and the Advanced Dentistry Accreditation Committee. He has been acknowledged by the United States 33rd Congress with a Congressional Record Award and has received citations for his commitment to community service from New York State Governor, New York State Assembly, and the Nassau County Executive.

Dr. Grant, his administrative staff, and hygienist have established a new state of the art office in Garden City, Long Island, NY, and a traveling dental team that provides dental service to persons who may be homebound or may reside at an assisted living facility, a senior center, a nursing home, or a rehabilitation facility. He is committed to providing the latest technology in dentistry, with an emphasis on cosmetic restoration and preventive dental care that is affordable.

Email	Drterrygrant1@gmail.com
Linkedin	linkedin.com/in/dr-terry-e-grant

AN ODE TO AUNT PERZELLA

by Dr. Terry E. Grant

As a "momma's boy," I viewed shopping with my mother as our special bonding time. When I was thirteen years old, my mother and I went off to go shopping on our favorite day of the year, Black Friday. During the car ride back home, I noticed that the clouds in the sky had an odd color, which gave me an unsettled feeling. As soon as we turned onto our block, the unsettled feeling I had in my chest bolted with sensation. My Aunt Perzella came running toward the car as my mom pulled into the driveway.

My aunt was crying. She said that my father had called an ambulance because my brother, Darren, was not breathing. She said that my father had just gone with the ambulance to the hospital about 10 minutes ago. My mother immediately backed out of the driveway and rushed to the Emergency Room entrance of our local hospital.

As we walked into the hospital, I spotted my father's eyes. At that moment, I knew our lives changed forever. My father embraced my mother and me with the tightest hug I'd ever felt, as he whispered to us that Darren had died.

My mother, in utter denial, spun around and screamed out at the emergency room doctor, "He's only eight years old!" Through her tears, she told the doctor that she had just taken Darren to the pediatrician four days ago.

Darren had been complaining of a sore throat, and the pediatrician had told my mother that she was an over-anxious parent. The emergency room doctor told my mother that Darren had undiagnosed rheumatic fever.

My dad consoled my mom, as her yelps rang through the emergency room halls. I ran outside, my chest still pounding with anxiety and disbelief. I needed fresh air. I called up to the sky and yelled to God. "Why did you take my favorite brother?" I asked him. Sometime later, my father found me outside the hospital and he told me that we needed to go home. When we got back to the house, I stayed on our front porch. I did not want to go into my bedroom, because it was one that I shared with Darren and it would make it more real that he was really gone. I cried and prayed. I made a vow that day to be a doctor, so that no other child or person would die from an undiagnosed condition.

My Aunt Perzella came outside to join me on the front porch. She was worried about me. Because of the fact that Darren and I shared the bedroom, she knew the close bond that we shared. I told her that I was going to be a doctor.

She sat me down and said, "Son, you can be whatever you want to be. You keep studying, but more importantly, you must make a plan and a path to follow. You must stay on that path, because your path is a gift from God and your path is only for you and you alone to follow. If, for any reason, a rock or anything gets in your path, then you must stop, look to God, your savior, and go around that rock or thing and continue on your path to success."

Upon my entrance into high school, I became interested in volunteering at medical offices. My family dentist, with an oddly similar last name to mine, Dr. Gant, allowed me to volunteer in his dental practice. Dr. Gant was an African American dentist and it was important for me to see a doctor that looked like me, especially at that age. His front desk dental assistant, Nurse Jessie, accepted me as if I were her own son. She was a very caring lady.

I would wake up early on Saturday mornings to volunteer at Dr. Gant's dental practice on the days that I did not have a team practice. Nurse Jessie would always greet me and tell me that I was blessed, which was a formidable aspect of my experience volunteering at the dental practice. After, she would give me her breakfast order to be picked up at the bodega across the street: a toasted roll with butter and a small coffee with one sugar.

I looked forward to volunteering at Dr. Gant's office so much that I would often get there before Dr. Gant or his assistants would show up. I enjoyed the times that I would sit in his office in between patients and he would impart his immeasurable wisdom upon me. I shared with him what my Aunt Perzella told me about never giving up your dream, regardless of what path you have to take, and to always know that God and the spirits of loved ones who passed on will stay with you.

Dr. Gant would often say that my Aunt Perzella was right on point. He often said to me, "Terry, you could do this too. Dentistry is an art and a science. Since you are good in math and science and your dad is an artist, I believe you will be a fine Doctor of Dentistry." I guess we can say that Dr. Gant was that power of one with that statement.

Don't get me wrong. I had very supportive parents that fostered my drive. My mother was very nurturing. She opened a daycare center inside our home. My father instilled the drive and motivation in me to make the very man I am today. My dad was a proud man and was a true leader inside and outside our home. He served as a union representative on his job at Singer Sewing Company. I distinctly remember meeting Congresswoman Shirley Chisholm at a rally held at Yankee Stadium when the many local unions were endorsing her, and my dad wanted to make sure that I attended the rally. My dad often worked two jobs. He would come home from his day job and sit with the family around the dining room table for dinner, as we would discuss the events of our day. Afterward, he would take a short nap and get up to get ready to go to his second job. Observing my father's extreme work ethic to provide for his family gave me the foundation to motivate myself to complete my journey. Both my dad's stellar work ethic and Dr. Gant's mentorship were monumental in my pursuit for a career in dentistry.

The summer before I entered college, my Aunt Perzella fell ill. She was diagnosed with terminal cancer that she hid from our family. She passed away just as I entered my freshman year of college. This was a massive loss to me as we had a truly close bond, but I was determined to start college on the right foot. I registered for classes in my first semester and focused on a pre-dental school curriculum, which included Biology, Inorganic Chemistry, Calculus, and African American Art History.

The college experience was a bit daunting, as I was away from my friends and family and just overall felt like I was outside my league. I tried to make friends by overextending myself in extracurricular activities, as I joined the football and wrestling teams. My overextension was truly reflected in my first semester grades. I received three D's and a B. I arrived home for Christmas break with my suitcase filled with emotions and shame, as I felt like I had disappointed my family.

I told my parents about my grades and struggles with my first semester classes. My dad immediately contacted a family friend, Dr. Greta Rainsford, for assistance in helping to motivate me to get back on track. She invited my dad and me to her home. She asked me to sit next to her and she looked me deep into my eyes, as if she knew my heart.

She said, "Terry, you just have to work harder. Drop all those extracurricular programs and focus only on your schoolwork because that is why you are in college. Your classmates are not smarter than you; it's just that they received a head start to the information that you are just now being taught. You will have to work harder to learn the information first and then study to memorize it to show that you understand everything. You should not let money get in the way of getting the resources you need to learn. All libraries have a reservation department, where the professors put textbooks on reserve. You can easily go to the library and read the additional textbooks that are on reserve."

When the winter break concluded, I was recharged and invigorated by my parents' and Dr. Rainsford's words. I returned to campus and found a room in the library basement that was not being used on a daily basis and that became my new office. I found that studying in this room, and not back in my dorm room with the variety of distractions, assisted me in raising my grades. Soon thereafter, I was averaging A's and B's and eventually made the Dean's list.

When I made the Dean's List, I brought the certification to my Aunt Perzella's gravesite. I kneeled and prayed over her tombstone. As I stood up, I found two $20 bills lying at my feet. I immediately came home to tell my mother what had taken place. My mother said Aunt Perzella was so proud of you and her spirit found a way to reward you. It felt like they were all pieces of a puzzle in my life that put me on the path that my Aunt Perzella had often spoken to me about. I actually did not understand it then, but I do understand it now. I know that, in heaven and on this earth, my Aunt Perzella is proud of me and all my accomplishments to date. I am Dr. Terry Grant, and she knows that her words never forsook me.

◆◆◆◆◆◆◆ ABOUT ◆◆◆◆◆◆◆

Rev. Dr. Phil Craig

Rev. Philip Craig was ordained an AME elder at *The Greater Allen AME Cathedral of New York* under the leadership of the Senior Pastor, the Honorable Rev. Dr. Floyd H. Flake, and Co-Pastor, Rev. Dr. Elaine M. Flake. He is currently the pastor of the Greater Springfield Community Church [aka GSCC], one of the fastest growing churches in Southeast Queens.

Rev. Craig is a known community activist and organizer, motivational speaker, prolific preacher, church consultant, husband, father, and, most of all, servant of the most High God. He currently serves on a number of boards locally and nationally. Rev. Craig possess a Certificate in Christian Ministry, Associate degree in Applied Science, Bachelor's degree in Organizational Management, Master's degree in Business Administration, Master's degree in Divinity, and a Doctoral degree in Ministry.

Rev. Craig says he values all his roles and accomplishments, but the one he cherishes the most is the opportunity to serve God and His people. He continues to reside in Jamaica, Queens with his lovely wife Jennifer and three beautiful children Jasmine, Christina (aka "CC"), and Jonathan-Philip Craig.

Email	philcraigspeaks@gmail.com
phone	718-528-9539
Instagram	@pcspeaks
Twitter	@philcraigspeaks
Facebook	@phil.craig.505

ABUNDANT LIFE AFTER A HEART ATTACK

by Rev. Dr. Phil Craig

I believe that success or failure is ultimately our choice. From the beginning of time, God has always given his people the power of choice. It is always our choice where reward or consequence manifests in our lives. On June 6, 2019, I was faced with a choice when I received a call from my doctor's office saying that I had had a heart attack. I had just taken a stress test earlier that day. I would never forget that feeling. In that moment, my entire body went numb. I was in a total state of shock. I never thought I would have heard those words from my doctor "Mr. Craig, you had a heart attack."

For a moment, I had thought there was a possibility that they'd gotten the medical records mixed up. So, my initial response to the doctor was to repeat my name to make sure they got the right records and were talking to the right person. The doctor reassured me that she was speaking to the right patient and had diagnosed me as already having had a heart attack. I also had a major blockage in my main coronary artery. She said that if I did not get to the hospital as soon as possible I might have another heart attack that could be fatal.

Even at that point, I was still in denial. It wasn't until I saw how persistent the doctor was, by calling me three times within 30 minutes to make sure I was on my way to the hospital for an emergency angioplasty procedure, that it sunk in.

One of the worst feelings in the world is to be lying in a hospital bed being prepped for surgery and not knowing what they will find or what the final results will be. If I could turn back the hands of time, knowing what I know now, I would, without a doubt, do things differently. First and foremost, I would have been more conscientious about my food intake. Second, I would have taken my pre-medical alerts more seriously. For example, when I was told my cholesterol, blood pressure, and glucose levels were high, instead of leaving the doctor's office thinking everything was going to work out on its own, I would have addressed my issues immediately. I am a firm believer that knowledge is power, but I also know many of us may have the knowledge but that's only have the battle. Having the knowledge and not applying it is useless.

I recall feeling, on that day in June as I sat in the recovery room immediately after my first procedure, that there is life after a heart attack because the choice was mine and I was determined to choose life and not death. As a spiritual advisor, I found myself in a position now to take some of my own advice that I had given to others apply it to my own life during that time of crisis. This was a chance for me to utilize the words in my head that I had recommended to so many others to help them to get through their crises to now help me get through mine.

As a person who has been diagnosed with diabetes, hypertension, high cholesterol, high triglycerides, and now a heart attack, I came to the realization that I needed to make some permanent changes if I wanted to bounce back and live a long, healthy life. Life after a heart attack requires two things to be done to secure a promising future. *Restore* and *Revive* should be the priority after a heart attack.

Restore means to bring back or to reinstate. The bottom line is: when your body has taken a hit like a heart attack, your first step is to restore your body as much as possible to your normal operating system before your trauma. After a heart attack, so many questions are racing through your mind. Questions like: How bad was my heart attack? How long before I'm able to get back to my normal routine? And last but not least, the question every heart attack victim would like to know is: Will I be able to live a normal life after a heart attack?

All these questions have a common answer. That answer is: "It depends on you." Your doctor may have told you to be sure to take the medicine that was prescribed, and I would recommend you do so, but at the same time, you should look at what would be best for your body during your recovery season.

The first thing you will need to do is to try and remove as many toxins from your body as possible. I am a firm believer that the body has the ability to repair itself when it's given natural resources that nourish its healing abilities. In order for the body to heal itself, it would need some help from you. For starters, if you're a smoker, you would need to stop smoking. Eating organic vegetables and fruits would begin to fuel your body with the necessary nutrients to get you started. Regular exercise was also a part of my restoration process. After praying and fasting, the plan God gave me was a plan that I believe was not for me to keep to myself.

So, today I share with you not only my testimony but also a sensible template for not only healing from whatever incident you may have incurred but for thriving and reversing your condition. Many Americans suffer from heart conditions, but they also suffer from a lack of knowledge. Knowledge can make the difference between either saving or losing your life. What I have found is that most hospitals do not give any more information to heart attack victims like myself, other than to eat a low-fat diet that includes more grains and fiber. Additionally, many, if not all, heart attack victims are also given blood thinners and a cholesterol medicine, as the doctors claim that will help toward healing. In my understanding, cholesterol medicine can deplete an enzyme called CoQ10 that strengthens the heart. In December 2008, I began taking a cholesterol medicine to lower my cholesterol and by January 2009, I was on an operating table getting a catheterization to see why, all of a sudden, my heart was having severe arrhythmia issues. I never suspected that the medicine given to me to help me could actually do me more damage. Then I came across a blog and read about dozens of other patients who were taking this same cholesterol lowering medicine and experiencing the exact same symptoms I had begun to experience. Now I don't have the scientific data to claim this would happen to everybody, but it did teach me to do better research on medicine and the foods that I put into my body.

As you recall, I recently mentioned that part of your restoration process should be to eat organic vegetables. I say this with the emphasis on the word *organic*. During my research in trying to get my body in a more suitable position to make a comeback, I discovered that conventional vegetables may not be as good for the body as you may think. Conventional fruits and vegetable can be doing more harm than good. A study done in October 2018 found that eating organic foods can contribute to lowering cancer risks. The researchers found that the study participants who consumed organic foods most frequently had 25 percent fewer cancers across all types when compared with people who never ate organic foods. A few studies have reported that organic produce has higher levels of vitamin C, certain minerals, and antioxidants, which are thought to protect the body against aging, cardiovascular disease, and cancer.

When it came down to my health, I didn't want to just get back to a normal place with it, I wanted to thrive. I wanted to be better than how I had been before. I wanted to be able to keep up with my children, especially my eight-year-old son, who has all the energy in the world. I had something to prove. I had a score to settle with statistics. I was determined that if God had allowed me to be part of the 6% who survives a heart attack like mine, then there had to be a reason why He had spared my life. I believe my life wasn't spared just for my own good but also for the good of others who would listen to my testimony. Making a comeback, in any instance, would not be easy, but it would be possible.

One of my favorite scriptures in the bible is: "I can do all things through Christ that strengthens me." It is with His guidance that I have been able to discern what is actually good for my body and what is not. Although I don't promote this, there were times when I had to take myself off medicines that doctors put me on as I felt they were doing my body more harm than good. After the first three to six months of my restoration process, it was time for me to bump it up a level or two. My doctor said I was losing weight, I looked healthy, and my tests were all looking good, so I was able to increase my exercise regimen from 15 min of cardio a day and 30-minute walks to 30–40 minutes of cardio daily and 30-minute walks.

It's much easier when you can find a solution that will make your exercise and walks interesting. During the summer, while my son was out of school, he would walk with me and that would make our walks to go by faster. When I was working out in the gym, I would work out to my favorite music playlist and watch movies on my phone to make the time go by faster. The key to my success was consistency. I must admit, when I stopped going to the gym during the holiday season, I felt my body going through transition that wasn't pleasant.

What I learned is that your body becomes conditioned to how you treat it. Once you begin to feed your body good food and regular exercise, you will feel a negative effect if you ever go back to unhealthy habits you moved away from. It was at this point that I knew I didn't want to go back to where I came from. I didn't like the feeling of sluggishness, bloating, and fatigue from fueling my body with unhealthy foods, and I didn't want to ever go back on the operating table or spend days in the Emergency Room in the hospital anymore. So, my next step was to walk into a revival experience regarding my health.

The definition of the word **Revive** is "to regain life or give new strength or energy to." Life after a heart attack can cause depression, but I'd come to believe that it was time now for a revival regarding my health. The first thing I did was to make sure I was spiritually sound and had a long talk with God. Scripture says "*Do not be anxious about anything*, but in every situation, by prayer and petition, with thanksgiving, present your requests to God." Prayer, for me, keeps me focused. Prayer, for me, keeps me grounded, simple minded, and able to remove all the distractions from my life that could keep me from obtaining my success.

Revival in the spiritual realm is to get that new strength while walking by faith that will allow you to climb over every mountain in your path when God decides to not move them. What helped me in this revival season was to look at my progress. I am a firm believer that any goal you set in life needs to be written down and kept visible. When you write it down and keep it visible, you are more likely to put it into action. In my case, my goals were to lose 40 pounds in eight months. In order to accomplish this, I would have to average a loss of five pounds per month.

In the beginning, we get excited and go strong to obtain our goals and we do good for a little while, but then we drop off. But when we keep our goals in front of us, we won't forget what we need to do. What worked for me was to keep my progress in a little black book in which I recorded my weight and what I ate each day. This allowed me to see if I lost my way temporarily and to get right back on track. Our revival reason is not to obtain the health we had before the tragedy, but to reach the health that is going to allow us to do things above and beyond what we can imagine or think. When we want to soar in a revival state, we can't compare ourselves with the normal. Going from restoration to revival is place where we go from standing to flying. A question I needed to ask myself was: Do I just want to stand or do I want to fly? Do I want to experience the normal or the paranormal? Do I want to be common or uncommon?

When we enter into a revival state of mind, our thinking and perception of life must change. How we view ourselves is how we take care of ourselves. When we look at ourselves as being priceless, we will take care of ourselves as if that was the case. We have been wonderfully made by God, and He intends for us to take care of ourselves accordingly. We are to present ourselves as a living sacrifice, as pure and perfect as possible.

Since the heart attack, I have come to the realization that my life isn't my own. It belongs to my creator, and my job is to be the best steward over this body that I can be. So, my vow to myself and to my creator is that, in spite of the past, I can become greater in the future. So, if I had to leave you with anything as my closing remarks, I would advise you to always be RELENTLESS. Never giving up, and never give in. If God did it for me, truly he can do it for you.

٠ ٠ ٠ ٠ ٠ ٠ ٠ ABOUT ٠ ٠ ٠ ٠ ٠ ٠ ٠

Milton Shelton Jr.

Milton Shelton Jr. is a man of God and a humble servant who desires to inspire. He is a son, a brother, an uncle, a father, and a grandfather. He is a native New Yorker who resides outside of Atlanta, Georgia. He is committed to supporting the mental health and substance abuse communities. He has worked diligently in these two fields for almost three decades, as well as working for several years in the correctional/ probation/ parole system. He sincerely believes that his purpose is to help as many people as possible. He feels called to do what he does and realizes to whom much is given, much is required. It is his philosophy that if a person can change the way they think, they can change their life. It is his desire to support total wellness of mind, body, and spirit and to serve God through his work in his community.

Email	milton157@att.net
Phone	(678) 577-2909
Facebook	www.facebook.com/Clain617

STAGE 5

by Milton Shelton Jr.

It was December 9, 2014, and the doctor said, "You have stage four cancer, sir, and we need to treat it quickly and aggressively."

Initially, it didn't even register in my mind correctly. I thought to myself, "Wait… What did he just say?" I had never even imagined the lump on my neck would be diagnosed as a cancerous tumor. I had always been healthy. Then, shock and fear quickly seeped into my existence, totally consuming me. How else can one take such dreadful news?

A young African female nurse took me and my family into a room, where she prayed with us. Immediately, I was directed to God and by a complete stranger. So much for the holidays, as Christmas and New Year's Day became just two regular days to me. I was shook!

Treatment was scheduled for early January, and I must admit, fear of the unknown seemed to grow with each new day. It was determined, by total strangers, that the best treatment would be radiation and chemotherapy. I really didn't think that I could do what they were prepping me for. I wasn't ready. This wasn't fair. *Why me? Why now?*

"What if I refuse treatment?" I asked.

A white female doctor replied, "The cancer will probably enter your lungs and you will die a slow, ugly death."

My 19-year-old first-born son, Milton III, said, "You have to do this. I need you for at least ten more years."

Then, without hesitation, my 16-year-old baby boy, Milano, chimed in, "I need you for at least 20 more years, Pop."

It was as if God himself was speaking to me through them. It was just what I needed to hear from the two people who mattered the most in my life. That settled it. I had to fight the dreaded disease. I was their leader and couldn't let my soldiers see me surrender. I knew I might die, but it was important to me for my sons to see and know I fought until the end.

January and February might as well have been renamed Chemotherapy and Radiation for me. I had chemotherapy every two weeks for a total of four times. A needle was inserted into my hand, and the anti-cancer drugs were injected for several hours each time. This treatment was relatively easy for me, but the lasting side effects were awful. They made it seem as if the doctors had shot poison into my veins. First of all, for several months, it felt like someone was sticking a straight pin into the tips of my ten fingers and ten toes. Also, my hearing was amplified for certain sounds, which was like torture to me. The shower water was the main sound I could not bear. I was forced to take three-minute showers because it was just too loud in there. I could not take the volume. The rattling of a potato chip bag was another sound I couldn't tolerate. It was so loud, but to only me, that I actually wanted to hurt someone for eating their bag of potato chips. My ears had become so super sensitive that I tried to live in silence every chance I got.

Radiation to me was like getting burned in the same exact spot 35 different times. There was no heat or flame that could be seen or felt though. The wound progressively became bigger and worse each time, and by the end of 35 sessions, I had a huge, open, ugly scar on the side of my neck. It looked like someone had burned me with a blowtorch. I also had a massive wound inside my throat. First, they made a mask that went around my head and shoulders. I insisted that they not cover my face, so they cut the face out. This mask, which I wore each day for radiation treatment, was made out of hard plastic and was fastened to a table that I had to lie on for five minutes as this huge machine circled my head. Once they fastened the mask to the table,

I could not move at all. Not being able to move terrified me. Being in that big room, alone, with that big machine terrified me. I quickly realized I had claustrophobia. It felt like I was lying in a casket and my natural reaction was to escape, but I couldn't move and the fear and panic was real. Five minutes seemed like forty-five, and I struggled greatly for the first two days. Just as my doctor was prescribing me some medication to allow me to relax, my sister Sharon Quinn just happened to send me a song on my phone titled "I Am" by Jason Nelson. I love that song, because it was so calming in my chaos. I asked if the song could be played during my treatments.

Every morning thereafter, the young people who treated me by operating the machine from another room had the song cued up and ready as I entered the room. I feel God sent me those young people to encourage and inspire me, which they did well. It was a young black woman and two young men, one Caucasian and one of Indian descent. They were all angels to me. As that song played 33 more days, I was able to relax long enough to receive the treatments without the medicine. I remember instead of lying there helpless, panicking, and fearing death, I focused on the song and felt God's presence in the room with me. Just us two. Yes, he was most definitely there with me.

Every day my fear was controllable now, for five minutes a day, five days a week, for seven weeks. I credit that song because I couldn't relax without it. It gave me hope. Ironically, the artist even mentioned cancer in the song. I later reached out to Mr. Nelson to thank him personally. He seemed genuinely happy that his song had helped me to overcome my medical issue. It was all love.

During my two months of daily treatments, things continued to get worse. This is going to sound unbelievable, but trust me: I couldn't make this up. On January 9th, I ate some food my coworkers had prepared during an office party. I couldn't taste it at all. It seemed like I was just chewing and swallowing cardboard. I immediately knew it was the chemo. Just like that, my taste buds were inoperable. Chemo killed my taste buds completely. Can you imagine eating your food but it has no taste? None! Zero flavors! I couldn't taste the difference between veggies, fruits, meats, fish, or anything. They were all tasteless. The only difference was in the textures of the foods. This part I really hated so much that I voluntarily stopped eating. Why even bother?

No flavor or taste made it worthless to me. That was the last day I ate any food until May 10th, four months later. For the next five to six weeks, I had no nourishment at all. I lost 80 pounds in six weeks and literally forgot what being hungry even felt like.

Let me repeat that. I wasn't even hungry, and I forgot what it was like to be hungry. If I had not lived it, I probably wouldn't believe it myself. I still wonder, "How did I survive?" As the scar inside my throat progressively became worse from the radiation, I quickly became unable to swallow anything. Originally, I stopped eating because it was no longer enjoyable without any flavor or taste, but now I was truly unable to eat even if I wanted because I could no longer swallow.

I was starving and dehydrated. I had what had to be the hugest and ugliest scar ever on my neck, and I went from 265 pounds to 180. My hair fell out and I was now bald. I looked like death. I could see the reactions of my friends. One even broke out in tears at the sight of me. I could see that they saw a dead man walking.

After about 30 radiation treatments, I had enough. My young white radiation doctor said I owed her just five more treatments because I'd missed a couple during holidays. I insisted that I only owed her three, but the truth is, I knew she was right. I just couldn't stand the pain anymore. Mentally and physically, I had quit. I tried, but I couldn't take anymore. The morphine didn't work anymore. Neither did the oxycodone, and the pain patches were useless too. I was always drugged up and couldn't stay awake for long. I was tired of it all and ready to die.

I told the doctor this, and I guess she told my family and then the call came from New York. It was my oldest sister, Dr. Cheryl James. She quickly three-way-called my sister Sharon and their words were, "You've come too far to give up now. Man up and push through it. What's five more treatments?" They both tried me! They challenged my manhood and tested my gangster like only they could.

My sisters are two tough Brooklyn-born chicks who have always made me a better man. Steel sharpens steel. I've never been sweet, soft, or scared. But this cancer was nothing nice. Truthfully, I was terrified. I didn't think I'd make it, and I didn't care anymore until speaking with my sisters. They gave me back what I had lost that last week, which was the desire to fight to the finish. I'm forever indebted to them for that.

I am also very much indebted to my lady at that time. My better half. I won't reveal her identity here and now, but she knows who she is. She attended all those daily hospital visits with me for months, and I will always love her for that. I could not have done it without her either. Another strong woman who kept my spirits as high as possible while nursing, chauffeuring, and constantly encouraging me that everything will be alright. She weathered the storm and put up with all of my crazy. Another angel God sent to me. I salute you, Queen.

Lastly, I am indebted to my praying Mother who had a host of prayer warriors lifting me up. I come from a praying family. My grandparents made sure of that. My mom's prayers have been covering me all my life. Those prayers have rescued me many times over my years. The power of prayer is undeniable. When I count my many blessings, I count my mother twice. Thanks, Ma.

The last week of treatment, I thought I was going to die. I was scared to go home, so I checked myself into the hospital. If I was going to complete this last week of radiation, I had to stay there. I had become too weak. I could barely walk and couldn't talk. I wrote all my communication on paper for the family and medical staff that last week. If I was going to die, it was going to be in the hospital and not in the house with my son.

It was at that last chemo session that I met a woman whose husband was also being treated. She told me to consider a feeding tube for nourishment. She said it had made a big difference in her husband's recovery. My chemo doctor happened to be an Oriental male who said that during recovery I had to drink four Ensure or Boost drinks daily for nourishment and to regain strength. I knew I couldn't swallow my own spit by then, so I reluctantly requested the feeding tube.

The next day, I remember being wheeled on a gurney into an operating room, being put on a table, and given meds. A young black man spoke to me in that room and assured me that I was going to be all right. Another angel. The last thing I remember is being pierced in the stomach by a long piece of sharp metal and hearing myself moan as loud as I could. I quickly passed out and woke later that night with a feeding tube inserted directly into my stomach. I would pump three Ensures through that tube daily for the next three months.

All that I described was happening simultaneously for the entire two months of treatment and then some. Then the healing and recovery time began. I wouldn't return to a normal lifestyle for about six more months. I was in constant pain and discomfort while my wounds healed, both inside and outside. I continued to take minimal medication for fear of addiction. Most of the medicine I never even used or only used once. Some of it would put me into a deep sleep, and that was too close to death for me.

The physical scars are for life. I slowly began to get stronger, thanks to the Boost and Ensure, which I pumped directly into my belly through the feeding tube. During this time, I became fascinated watching two cooking shows on YouTube. I watched them nonstop, learning new techniques and recipes to use in the future because eating was impossible then. Anticipation kept me fully intrigued.

During treatment and recovery, I drove my son to school and picked him up after school every day, while sometimes nodding off to sleep at red lights. But I wanted to spend as much time with him as possible while I faced my own mortality. My oldest was away, fulfilling his military obligations.

A white German female doctor said I looked good with the weight loss. I kind of smiled again for the first time. Another white American female doctor told me that most chicks dug guys with scars. She made me feel good about myself.

On Mother's Day 2015, I attended church with my mom. Afterward, we went to a restaurant for breakfast. I decided to see if I could, and I swallowed a couple of teaspoons of grits and eggs. Ma later told me that seeing me eat again was the best Mother's Day gift ever.

I finally saw a little light at the end of the tunnel and felt that my life could eventually become normal again. A childhood friend would soon introduce me to juicing fresh vegetables and fruits, which are both high in cancer-fighting antioxidants. I had the feeding tube removed soon after.

Fast forward, four and a half years. I still juice daily. I eat healthier and exercise regularly. I kept the weight off and wear my scar proudly. Soon, I will have my annual appointments with both my chemo and radiation physicians. It will mark five years cancer free and will officially end all follow up tests and exams. I never ever have to go back. Never ever! God is good and miracles do happen. I'm going to ring that bell until it breaks.

Back when I thought about my stage four cancer, I'd think there wasn't a stage five. Why isn't there a stage five and six? In my mind, death came after stage four. And, unfortunately, it does for some. So, death was stage five to me.

During my journey I saw thousands of other cancer patients, and I know some didn't survive their fight. Sometimes, second chances never come. I saw people from all walks of life fighting. All ages. Even toddlers barely walking were fighting for their lives. Can you imagine chemo and radiation before you ever make it to pre-K? Before you learn the alphabet and to count? I saw all ages, all races, all sexualities, all religions, and all nationalities. All human beings. Cancer doesn't discriminate. It actually unites people.

That is why I made sure to describe all the people who personally helped me by their race, age, sex, and nationality in this story. I wanted to show how something so bad could produce something incredibly good. People helping people. Love doesn't discriminate either.

When I was at my worst, God's grace was at its best, and he sent me angels and most of them looked nothing like me. All I could see was loving, caring, kind, and gentle people there to assist me when I needed it the most. They all seemed to go way above and beyond their job requirements to accommodate me. The good people at the Winship Cancer Institute of Emory University are called and chosen. They are extraordinarily gifted. They rock!

Today, I notice the smallest gestures that I used to overlook. I find new value in things that I previously wouldn't even pay attention to. My perspective has shifted, and I have started to re-evaluate what was really important and many of my priorities have changed. I look at life totally differently, realizing that time is my greatest commodity. I can't get more time, so I have to make the absolute most out of each day now. I won't waste it.

I've stopped allowing foolishness to upset me as much. I'm quicker to forgive today. I'm more compassionate. My peace is priceless, and I won't let anyone disturb it. I don't entertain drama or negativity. I don't take life as serious anymore. I let my little boy come out and act silly. I sing and dance and don't care who's listening or watching.

I don't take anything for granted anymore, because I know it can all change in seconds. I cherish the moments. I take more chances and risks, because fear cannot be present where there is peace and love. Fear is not from God.

I'm more considerate and thoughtful. I'm more grateful and appreciative than ever. I know I'm blessed each morning I wake up. I create my own happiness and wear it daily. I recognize the little things. Most importantly, my personal relationship with God is at an all-time high and my faith is much, much greater. Cancer taught me to become a better person. In all my suffering and pain, my vision became much clearer.

The moral of this all is: Please don't let some dreadful disease or condition have to happen to you or yours to make you better. Re-evaluate yourself and your priorities. Money can't fix cancer. Stop stressing the small stuff. Don't waste time. Create your happiness and live there. Forgive others. Let it go and find peace. Be grateful and spread love.

And last, but not least, feed our similarities and starve our differences. Sex, race, and religion doesn't really matter when it's life and death. Love is love. My perception of stage five transformed as well. Today, stage five means life to me, not death. Life in abundance. Stage five is here and now. Stage five is a second chance. It is living my life to the fullest and giving back. Stage five is a positive attitude and good vibes. It is hugs and smiles. It is fearlessness. Stage five is sharing my story. Stage five is meeting Ma at church on Sunday morning. It is fishing with my grandsons and playing with my granddaughter and her dolls. Thank the Lord for stage 5.

⬩⬩⬩⬩⬩⬩⬩ ABOUT ⬩⬩⬩⬩⬩⬩⬩
Phil Andrews

Phil Andrews is the current president of the Long Island African American Chamber of Commerce, Inc. (LIAACC) and the president-emeritus of the Black Public Relations Society-New York. He is also a two-term past president of the 100 Black Men of Long Island. He is a member of the United Black Men of Queens, Inc. and sits on the President's Council of the Big Brothers and Sisters of Long Island.

Phil's work has been featured in multi-platform publications, including *Black Star News, The New York Beacon, Amsterdam News, Minority Business Review, New York Trend Newspaper, Southeast Queens, Scoop, The Village Press Online, Cision* "Behind the Headlines, *The Network Journal,* and more. He has also appeared on WABC *Here and Now* and NBC's *Positively Black.* He is also featured in the book *15 Years of Minority Business Development.* He is the recipient of the 2019 Small Business Champion award from the U.S. Small Business Administration's NY District Office. Throughout his career, he has received a host of citations from several notable political officials and has served on several boards.

He was born and raised in Brooklyn, and attended Brooklyn Technical High School. He served for several years in the US Navy and Army Reserves, and he attended York College and John Jay College. He graduated from paralegal school and had a nearly twenty-year career in law enforcement. Phil Andrews's goals involve encouraging as many promising young men as possible by compelling them to serve with the very best of their minds and talents.

Phone	347.475.7158
Website	www.liaacc.org
Twitter	mobile.twitter.com/philandrews
Linkedin	linkedin.com/in/liaacc-chamber-of-commerce-126351a2/
Facebook	m.facebook.com/LongIslandAfricanAmericanChamber/
Instagram	instagram.com/phil_andrews_pres/

THE MAKING OF A CHAMPION

by Phil Andrews

Everyone has the makings of a champion in them. It is something that is innate in all human beings. There is a popular saying that champions are made, not born. I believe that statement has some merit to it. Today, I share my personal experiences of bringing out the champion in my own life. It is my hope that sharing my experiences will help bring out the champion within you.

I grew up in the Marcy Housing Development. And, yes, that is the same housing complex where rapper Jay Z lived. I feel fortunate that I was raised in a loving environment, despite the loss of my mother at an early age. When my mother died, all my brothers and sisters who were not adults got placed in loving homes, which consisted of mostly relatives. This was a both a miracle and a blessing in disguise, as well as a great testament to the importance of family and community.

My twin sister Phyllis Andrews and I were raised by my Aunt Rev. Frances Virginia Young, who was a God-fearing woman full of integrity, wisdom, character, faith, and commitment to God. Aunt Francis was an evangelist of Grace Gospel Tabernacle, which was a small local church located between Park Ave. and Nostrand Ave. in Bedford Stuyvesant. It was a beacon of light in the community, where we learned the power of grassroots leadership. The lessons learned during this time also taught me the power of participation, which I adhere to up until this day, as I believe that every human being must stand up for what they believe and that being active in the affairs of society matters.

It was at Grace Gospel Tabernacle that I received early training in leadership development strategies. One of my fondest memories as a youth was being selected to go to Camp Joharie, run by Bethel Gospel Tabernacle under the leadership of Bishop Roderick R. Caesar, Sr. I was an inner-city kid, so going to a camp in the country was an experience that stayed with me for the rest of my life. At Camp Joharie, I enjoyed going on hay rides and participating in a pancake eating contest, which I won. This was one of my first experiences of being a champion.

Because of church, my sister and I were well versed in theology and reading. Anyone in my family would tell you that anywhere you saw me, I always had a book in my hand. I was fascinated by books. I believed they could take us to places that we had never been. I also believed that champions should embrace the concept of lifelong learning. It is said that one of the most important impacts on our lives is the books that we read.

Today, we no longer have to go the library to read, as we can read on our Kindles, iPads, computers, and cell phones, and we have the ability to have way more books in our hands than our ancestors did. Champions fully embrace the use of technology and find positive ways to use technology to enhance their educational achievements. I was fortunate to be exposed to *Think and Grow Rich* by Napoleon Hill at the age of 21, as well as other books on how to build world class companies. A champion takes the time to add educational enrichment to their schedule. Busy executives can even buy books in the form of excerpts with all the key points outlined. Therefore, the executive only has to read the more salient points versus reading the entire book. So, there are no excuses for not reading.

I was a great student early on in life. I attended Brooklyn Technical High without having any preparation for the special admission test. Today, there is a lot of controversy around the validity of the special admission test for specialized schools in New York City. At Brooklyn Tech, my English teacher said I had an uncanny sense of using and organizing words, and she went on to say to me that if I read everything from A to Z, I would become a great writer. Needless to say, I heeded her advice and embraced the concept of reading books from beginning to end.

Through sports, I learned the value of teamwork, hard work, persistence, practice, and setting goals in my life. In order for any person to become a champion, they must look at their assets. In the business world, there is an analysis called "SWOT," which stands for Strengths, Weaknesses, Opportunities, and Threats. Let's talk a few minutes about these concepts: Strengths – What are you really good at? Weaknesses – What are you not so good at? Opportunities – What are your potential opportunities? Threats – What are some potential dangers that you face?

The problem with the SWOT analysis is that we must be brutally honest with ourselves, and we also need honest feedback from others to accurately review our blind spots. We should make it a positive, regular part of our life to do a SWOT analysis because, at different points in our lives, things change.

One of the things I learned early on in life was the power of being involved in the community at a local level. This is another lesson I learned from my Aunt Francis Virginia. Getting and staying involved in community could take on many forms, such things as being active in a local church, serving on board of directors for a nonprofit, working on a committee at a nonprofit, feeding the homeless, mentoring, and a host of other activities. When we get in involved in the community, not only does it benefit our lives, but it also benefits others. When it comes down to community involvement, I came up with my very own concept: "It is not enough to work on your job, you must also work in the community."

I believe this is one of the greatest steps to becoming a champion: starting right where you are in your local community to refine your championship skills. My mentors always today me, "Where our interests are at stake, we must be at the table" Being a participant in society gives an individual a sense of power and shows us that taking responsibility can help us obtain positive changes in our communities. That is the stuff that champions are made of in life.

Earlier, I mentioned serving on boards as something a champion can do, but we need to do more than just sit on a board. We need to "Show Up and Show Out." A champion brings his or her A game to all aspects of life.

It is a known fact that if you are a slacker on a board, then you will be a slacker in other parts of your life. Bad habits are easy to form and hard to break; good habits are hard to form and easy to break. Champions live by the concept of "Give your best to the world, and the world will give the best back to you." To some, this Championship law is known as the law of reaping and sowing. I served on boards, such as the Roosevelt Chamber of Commerce and West Indian Chamber of Commerce. I was also elected to the board of directors of a local chapter of 100 Black Men of America. It is not easy to lead the charge of engaging others to bring their A game to all of life's circumstances, but I did.

Champions also work though the law of seasons, because there are times in our lives when different things are happening but we still need the stuff inside us that inspires champions to go to the next level regardless of what is going on. One of my favorite quotes in life is: "Don't get to high on the ups, and too down on the downs. Life is about hanging in there, no matter what level you are on." Champions possess attributes, such as persistence, determination, a strong work ethic, integrity, emotional intelligence, and a host of other attributes that depend on the unique situations in their lives.

Champions are often the beneficiaries of mentoring. They also know and understand that "mentoring is the gift that keeps on giving." I have been fortunate to have become acquainted with some of the most outstanding men and women that society produces. However, I must say it was intentional that I met them, as I sought them out, mostly through networking.

Champions are advocate networkers. For many years, I ran a business networking group by the name of the Power Networking Business Series, and the idea behind the concept was to combine networking with Business Training, as I believe networking is fruitless without showing up with top notch business skills. People do business with people they Know, Like, and Trust. Therefore, you must be intentional about the people you associate with in your life and only associate with individuals who can help you to become more than what you are by being proactive. The book *Never Eat Alone* by Keith Ferrazzi explains it this way: " If you do something to make someone else more successful, they're more likely to value your relationship with them, and the more relationships you have with value in them, the more valuable you become, not only to yourself, but to the world: your employers, your clients, and so on. It is not important that you play golf, but what is important is the type of people you golf with should be people who can help you become more than what you are at this point in your life." Champions know that they have a need to engage others on the road to success. No man or woman is an island, and now one achieves substantial success without the help of others.

In May 2019, I was named by the New York District of The United States Small Business Administration as the 2019 Small Business Champion. The New York District Office covers 14 counties in downstate New York. This was primarily due to the work that I have done over the years helping small businesses as the current president of the Long Island African American Chamber of Commerce (LIAACC). God will always make room for your gifts, and since I've become president of LIAACC, our involvement in the community has empowered many to become successful in their business endeavors. Servant leadership has been talked about over the last couple of years, and several books have been published on the topic, but those principles have been around a very long time. The principles simply state that a person who wishes to be the greatest of them all must be a servant to them all. I have discovered that, in order to be a champion to more people, you must constantly look for ways and means to expand your impact on the territory that you serve. You must always look for ways to grow as a human being in all aspects of your life, and that is what makes me a champion and is what can make you one too.

✦ ✦ ✦ ✦ ✦ ✦ ABOUT ✦ ✦ ✦ ✦ ✦ ✦

Lee Scott Coleman

Lee is a native of New Orleans who currently resides in Zachary, LA. He is married to Cynthia London Coleman and will be celebrating their 29th year wedding anniversary in August. They have one son, Imani Coleman, who just turned 14 years old this past May. Lee is a military veteran and has received honorable discharges and various other awards from the Navy, Air Force, and Air National Guard. He retired from the Air National Guard as a Master Sergeant after serving 27 years. During his tenure in those different branches of the military, he served in the capacity of a Jet Engine Mechanic, Aircraft Mechanic, and Disaster Preparedness Technician.

Lee graduated from Southern University with honors, obtaining a Bachelor of Science in Secondary Education and a Master's Degree in Administration and Supervision. He has served as an educator for the 21 years, teaching at the elementary, middle, and high School levels. He was selected as Educator of the Year by the Kiwanis Club of Early Risers during his tenure as principal of Banks Elementary. He has also been an assistant principal at West Feliciana High, and is currently a district supervisor at West Feliciana Family Service Center. Although he is an accomplished public servant, his greatest joy is being a servant of our Lord and Savior Jesus Christ.

Email	coalman2003@gmail.com
Phone	225-658-2875
Facebook	facebook.com/lee.coleman.9849
Linkedin:	linkedin.com/in/ice3-lee-coleman-598736100/

DIVINE CONNECTION
by Lee Scott Coleman

It is stated that when a man finds a wife, he finds a good thing and obtains favor from the Lord. This is a common expression among church folk that you hear preachers say all the time. I've come to see it manifest itself firsthand, after almost thirty years of marriage. Reflecting to the beginning, the year was 1990 when I met my wife in the Airforce Reserve. It was a late afternoon, and I was a crew chief on an A10 Warthog aircraft. Cynthia was assigned to perform various maintenance duties on the bombing systems. It was her eyes and lips that caught my attention; there was an innocence and naiveté about her that led me to strike up a conversation. We talked that day and every day thereafter, the entire time she worked on the plane. We became good friends and often talked about everything. I remember telling my best bro that I had met a beautiful woman and that she was going to make someone a wonderful wife. It just was not going to be me.

I don't know why I said that, but then again, I do. I was running the streets, doing everything that I was big and bad enough to do. My heart was scarred and full of pain, which caused me to leave a trail of tears of broken-hearted women. I didn't feel good about myself, which is why I also didn't think I was good enough for her. My mind also told me not to get involved with her, because I would damage her for a future good man. Needless to say, we were married on August 31, 1991, and the very next day I was baptized in Jesus's name.

This is where the road starts to get curvy and bumpy. Just like many, I had a misconception about giving my life to Christ. I thought that everything would be good, perfect, and even peachy. My wife was not a worldly woman, and many would say she is holy. She had not been exposed to the things of the world, like I had been. I came into the marriage with baggage, carrying with me the spirits of dozens of women I had relations with. I had abused alcohol on and off for many years during my time in the military, and I found that spirit coming back into my life. I was a functional abuser of alcohol, often drinking by myself on many occasions. Drinking was my medication. I would never drink at home or in front of my family, so they didn't know that I would guzzle down three 24 oz. Red Dogs in less than an hour. There's a certain warmth about self-medicating with alcohol.

My wife and I had been married for 14 years. She'd had a miscarriage nine years back, so we didn't think we would ever have a child. However, on May 26, 2005, our son was born. There is nothing like the birth of a child. It took eighteen hours of labor for this miracle to come into the world. This moment had a profound impact on my life and helped me maintain stability and peace, both in my personal and professional life.

Just like any calm, a storm is close behind. I had just become principal of one of the most challenging elementary schools in the district. The job duties were overwhelming, and the challenges awakened the old man that I thought was long gone. I began slipping back into the old habits of drinking alone and away from home to handle the stresses. My family life suffered, and I was not giving my wife the attention that she deserved. My life was unraveling and spiraling out of control. I was holding on by the grace of God and just when you think it could get no worse, *BOOM* my wife left me.

Truly, this was the darkest hour of my life, but another blow soon would come. I would get the divorce decree, and my lovely wife wanted full custody of our son. This, my friend, was not going to happen. I snapped out of the spiral just enough to fight it in court and win. Joint custody, week to week, was given to both of us. I remember my wife saying that I wouldn't be able to take care of our son.

I replied, "You underestimate me. My mother raised a man."

I believe that the true measure of a man or woman is to be able to function in dual roles. Needless to say, I did it all. I brought him to daycare, fed him, and bathed him, and just overall loved on him. I do believe that this was a godsend, because I spent most of my time doing things with him. For nine months, we were in and out of courts. Separation is truly something I would not wish on anyone. The divorce was almost final, when out of the blue, my wife called and asked that we go on a retreat.

I said, "What do we need to go on a retreat for? This thing is over."

Guess what? I went, and my wife and I reconciled, and things were so much better. I still went off and on with mood swings, and after periods of going without, I would revert back to secretly sipping or, better yet, secret guzzling. The daily stresses of life and job would always suck me back up.

I remember I had taken a trip to Las Vegas and received a phone call from my doctor saying something was off with my last labs from a physical. I told the doctor I would get it checked out when I returned. I held off on the checkup until one day I went to the bathroom and my private parts swelled up to the size of a softball. I made an appointment immediately.

The retest of the labs ended up with the same results, and the data stated that I would have to go and see a urologist. So, thus began the journey of my life. The urologist didn't find anything, so he sent me to the blood specialist, then the heart specialist, then the kidney specialist. Here I was, reconciled with my wife and family, expecting the happy-ever-after and getting myself together. Well, the happy-ever-after would have to wait until at least I obtained results from the kidney specialist.

The kidney specialist came in all serious, so right off the bat I got a little nervous, but I felt really good, so I said to myself that there was nothing wrong with me. The doctor stated, "Mister Coleman, you have a massive growth on both of your kidneys, and it appears to be spreading to the other organs."

The first thing I thought was, "What do you mean growth?" For some reason, my mind reflected on a commercial. You know the one, where this couple are riding in the city. They are happy, smiling, having a good time, then

BOOM, bet you didn't see that coming! A car T-bones them on the side, and everything goes black.

Here it was that we had reconciled our marriage; everything was getting better and moving along. I had my wife back, son, and I was getting better and wiser, then BOOM!

Life is like that. Just when you think you have things going on, it has a way to bring you back down to earth. So, I was sitting in the nephrologist's office and I asked him," So, Doc, what's the prognosis?" Meaning what was the overall long and short-term outlook? Well what he said almost floored me.

He said, "You have six months to a year to live."

Now, they really didn't know what was wrong with me, but here he was saying that I will die in six months to a year.

I said, "You must be joking!"

He said, "This is what I see from what I have in front of me."

Being a student of the word and trying to be respectful, I said, "Well, doctor, no disrespect intended, but I don't receive that prognosis. I'm standing on the word of God, and his word says he promises me three score and ten years, which is 70 years old. Then it says I'll give you another ten years, which is for reasonable service, which would add up 80 years. I'm not close to 80, so I'm standing on the promise of God."

Thus began the journey of trials, tests, probing, prodding, and sticking. It took them sticking a 14-inch needle through my abdomen to the kidney to get a piece of it to find out that it wasn't cancerous. I would live and not die, but my faith would be tested beyond measure.

I believe God to be a healer, deliverer, an all-around miracle worker. So, I cried out to God for the healing. I had preachers pray for me, only to get to, "Why me?" My kidney function got down to 5%, and I had choices that had to be made. I either had to go on dialysis or have a kidney transplant. My circle of friends and family is fairly large, but no one stepped up to volunteer as a donor. No, not my wife, because I had told her I didn't want her to because she needed to be there for our son in case something happened with me.

The person that stepped up is a person I had known since I started teaching at the local high school. A Caucasian sister. It surprised me. We were sitting in a meeting and I had just given them the news about my situation, and she said, "Mister Coleman, I'll get tested."

Of course, I thanked her for the gesture but never took her up on it. I had lost a lot of weight and did not realize it until I saw a picture of myself. I looked like a stick man and couldn't believe it.

Everyone gets to what I call the turning point, a place where you have done all you could do, so now you just turn it over to Jesus. My wife told me she was going to go get tested. I told her I didn't want her to go get tested, and she knew why.

She stated to me, "Well, I'm going to get tested anyway."

I said, "Go ahead and get tested. You won't be a match."

Well, glory to God, she came back, shouting, "Perfect match, perfect match.!"

I asked her what she was talking about and she said that the doctors told her she was a perfect match to donate her kidney to me.

Anyone who has had a transplant knows that there are several factors that the health care professional test for to see if a person is a viable donor. In order for a person to donate any organ, three of the factors must match. The physicians told my wife that all the factors matched, so much to the point that we could be considered twins. It took me a week or two to reluctantly agree to go through the procedure over my concern for her. But this was a miraculous event, and I couldn't deny it. It was a blessing, and I just had to receive it.

We had the surgery on July 10, 2013, twelve days before my birthday. I remember my two sisters-in-law coming into the room and asking me how was doing. I told them I was just waiting for them to take me into surgery.

They burst out laughing, saying, "Man, you already had the surgery. You're in recovery."

The nurses came in and asked me if I want to go and see my wife. Another blessing. I mean up from the surgery the same day that I had it. We took the elevator up to her room to see her, and she was in more pain than I was. Having a transplant takes more out of the donor than the person receiving the organ. The recovery time of the donor is also longer than the person receiving the organ.

Fast forward to New Year's Eve 2013. We believe in bringing in the New Year at church. It is often said that what you're doing at the beginning of the year, you'll be doing at the end of the year. So, we came in with thanksgiving on our lips, praise in our hearts, and expectations that God was going to move. We praised God so hard everyone thought we would hurt ourselves, but nothing happened except the supernatural love of God. We got drunk in the spirit; the best high that anyone could possibly want to have. We left the church, came home, turned on the TV, and praised God some more. I remember our son running around praising God with us. What a time, what a time, what a time! This was the best New Year ever!

It is now 2020, and I haven't been sick or seriously ill in seven years. When I go for checkups, the doctors bring everyone around to see me. They all say it doesn't even seem like you have had a transplant.

I respond, "To God be the Glory."

The specialist said six months, but God said not so. I'm going to give him another chance. My wife, son, and I are in a great place. I'm free of all the stumbling blocks and shackles that held me in bondage for so long. Just think, 29 years ago I told a friend my wife was not for me. We got married, but we separated for nine months and were on the verge of divorce. I was given a death sentence, but God delivered me one more time.

I have a right to give Him praise and glory. God had a different plan for my life, His favor showed up and out. His grace and mercy snatched me from the valley of death for another opportunity to enjoy the abundant life. He was fighting my battles all the time. He said, in his word, I'll never leave you or forsake you. I'll be with you until the end of time. What the enemy meant for evil, God worked out for my good. God had appointed me since the beginning of time a DIVINE CONNECTION! When a man finds a wife, he finds a good thing and obtaineth favor from the Lord. Thank God for my FAVOR and a DIVINE CONNECTION!

So, to all those traveling on this journey called life: Don't get distracted by material things, status, and the overall rat race to the top. God has strategically placed people in our lives to see us through the valley experiences. Don't run from the valley, trials, or tests. Embrace them; it is there you will find your DIVINE CONNECTION.

* * * * * * * ABOUT * * * * * * *
Shawn D. Farnum

Shawn D. Farnum was born in Brooklyn, NY, and raised in Jamaica, Queens. He is a graduate of Lincoln University and a member of its 40 under 40. He has over 18 years of service as an educator, serving in the roles of teacher, dean, assistant principal, and principal. His entire career has been dedicated to uplifting and representing those who have no voice. He has accomplished much of this by working hard to staff schools and by hiring/training former students to work in his business. He founded Farnum's Finest Gourmet Desserts, based on his passion for food and a desire to create job opportunities for the young people he encountered throughout his career. These youth are also gingerly known as Farnum's Finest. He believes that the relationships we build, one interaction at a time or one dessert at a time, can change the world. Shawn is also a dedicated husband and father of four.

Email   farnumsfinest@gmail.com
Phone   (917) 382-3392
Linkedin   linkedin.com/in/ShawnFarnum
Website   www.farnumsfinest.com
Instagram / Facebook / TikTok / Twitter   @farnumsfinest

MY RECIPES FOR LIFE
by Shawn D. Farnum

The journey of a million miles begins with one step. Most are familiar with this phrase, but I would like to add something new to the world. All our lives are like a cake; whether good or bad, it comes down to the ingredients. When you think of the best cakes, cheesecakes, or desserts, we choose to use the highest quality ingredients available. The best flour, cocoa, etc. can be the difference between the best and the rest!

The first item I learned how to bake was a sweet potato pie. When I was seven, my mom wanted to keep me busy during the preparation for Thanksgiving dinner. I was given the responsibility for making dessert, and to me it wasn't really busy work as much as something I enjoyed doing. It allowed me to be close to my mom in ways that everyday life did not. The opportunity to connect with my mom in this way created some of the most loving memories I have.

These memories have become all the more important to me now, as my mom has developed severe memory loss over the last few years. The recipes I learned during these holidays have become important to my business, but even more as they stand as a beautiful reminder of the ingredients of life that I received from the best mom anyone has ever had.

I remember that first Thanksgiving, when I searched through all my mom's cookbooks to find my favorite sweet potato pie ideas. I synthesized parts of recipes from a few of the books to create my own, which stands to this day.

I made the pie the way that I wanted it to taste, and everyone that tasted it loved it. That was such a humbling experience that I have never forgotten.

I loved everything about the process of making sweet potato pies. I love choosing the ingredients, the smell while they baked, even the cooling time so I could dive in. But there is one thing in the sweet potato process I still dread every time I go through it: those darn threads!

The sweet potato is an amazing food source, and it makes a great dessert, but man those threads. Every sweet potato is held together by hundreds of super thin threads. These threads, if left in the mix, allow for great pie consistency but leave somewhat of an "after taste." So just take them out, right? Yes; but when you do that, the mix becomes watery. So, the threads are actually an ingredient within an ingredient.

The answer I came up with taught me a recipe for life. As we grow through life, we have experiences. This experiential learning process creates our own "threads," also known as our beliefs. These beliefs are unseen. They are created by the painful times, when we are abused or hurt by someone in our lives or seeing the family rock, my mother, where she is now. Our beliefs are created by joyful times, like the memories of time I spent with her in the kitchen. These beliefs, like the threads, can't completely be removed and they shouldn't be. To be clear with my message, the memories and experiences are not our beliefs. We choose to believe things based on what we experience in life.

So, what's the secret to my sweet potato pie? I remove as many threads as I can from my mix, but intentionally leave some behind. I also double the number of whole eggs, allowing the mix to stay smooth with no aftertaste. The consistency of the pie when baked is also excellent. The answer to the life threads or beliefs is the same. Beliefs are neither right nor wrong; some work for us, some don't. The ones that don't work must go, but in order for them to go, they must be replaced with beliefs that do work.

When I was molested as a child, I developed a belief that I should be ashamed. That shame belief kept me from developing loving, vulnerable relationships for a large portion of my life. But today, I choose a new belief. I'm a loving, vulnerable man who doesn't carry shame for something that happened 30 years ago. Life has become that much sweeter! We must choose our recipes. We must find what ingredients work for us and which ones don't. We must remove those that don't allow us to function and replace them with what will work. For sweet potato pie, I suggest more eggs. For your life, I suggest love for yourself and others. Love keeps everything together!

My recipe journey has been shaped by my time as an educator more than any other period in my life. An 18-year career as a dean, teacher, assistant principal, and principal is full of stories of the immense responsibility educators have in shaping the young people around us. These students spend more of their days in school than they do with their own families.

When I became a full-time teacher/dean at 22 years old, my understanding of the impact of life's challenges on children was truly amazing. I could actually see the complex issues that arose in school were always connected to some trauma/ingredient beyond our control. I started my career as a dean of students at a middle school in Queens, N.Y. The very first day of school was September 11, 2001. As you can imagine, there was chaos in the building that day. The destruction of the Twin Towers on that day shook the entire school community. However, the shaking was more like the sifting of the ingredients. I was given the leeway to change the common disciplinary approach to include a counseling and restorative focus. Students that got "in trouble" from that day forward were met with understanding and questions like," Why are you really sad, angry, and distracted? What can I do to help you? Who do you want to be because you are not what you have done or what was done to you?

This became my disciplinary application. I became a mentor, sounding board, motivator, standard bearer, challenger, father, older brother, and so much more. I became all things to all students, so I could get to the main ingredients and help guide them to creating their own recipes for life.

One of my favorite stories from my time at this middle school is a mentoring that has taught me about the chemistry of a recipe. I had a student at this middle school named "Robert." Robert was a handful. He was a walking, talking incident report. Robert had suspensions and troubles throughout his time in school. He loved a good argument but a fist fight even more! Man, he fought so much that, in a school of 2,000 sixth, seventh, and eighth grade students, my principal assigned me as Robert's personal dean! Any time Robert had any issues, I became the response, even when I was at home sick I would receive a phone call, and they would put him on the phone to be corrected. His actions eventually forced me to work with the school district to change his learning environment to another school setting.

Robert and I have stayed in contact. The mentor/mentee relationship continues. Many years after his time in school was over, he told me that anger was the ingredient that created the actions we saw. He told me he was molested as a kid and never told anyone but that he was so angry, hurt, ashamed, and sad that he had to get it out somehow. Robert is currently working in education; he is a married father of two and a mentor to innumerable students of his own. He is what become known in my world as one of Farnum's Finest, an example of what sharing love in the world can create. Robert's story is one example, but I have been blessed to have so many of these life recipe-changing experiences that when thinking up a name for the company that would express my love in the world in the food world, it became Farnum's Finest Gourmet Desserts.

When I was fired as a principal in 2015, I thought I had lost my purpose in life. My passion for pouring into the lives of young people seemed to be taken away. When the door closed, I fought hard to jar it open in so many ways. I received a text message from Robert a few weeks after I hadn't been working.

I told him about the circumstances and without a pause, he said," I was texting you to invite you to my graduation and now we have something else to celebrate!" He continued," Farnum, you have helped raise and impact so many people, including me, through junior high school, high school, incarceration, to graduating from college your words, and your life inspired me. It's time for you to impact the world through your entrepreneurial visions now."

Have you ever had a recipe changed by an unexpected ingredient? Robert added those ingredients that allowed me to begin working on my newest recipes.

Farnum's Finest, the food/dessert brand, was born in my mother's kitchen with the many love-filled recipes I learned from family and the friends of the family that visited our home from all over the world. The brand was raised in restaurants like Cornbread and Caviar in Long Island, NY and Chunn's Place in Hollis, NY. The depth and travel ability of the brand were developed at the first HBCU in the nation, Lincoln University, where I would cook and sell food in the kitchen/lounge of the Living Learning Center Dormitory. It was incorporated in the city of Queens in 2006, when I recognized after the birth of my first son that a legacy needed to be left through recipes. In all the years the company has been in existence, one thing is clear, and it is that the main ingredient in each recipe is love and we will not fail to accomplish greatness. This may not be the first time you have heard anything like this, but it is intended to be the FINEST.

Red Velvet Cake
- 3 cups flour
- 1.5 cups granulated sugar
- 1teaspoon salt
- 1 teaspoon baking soda
- 1/2 teaspoon baking powder
- 1 teaspoon Dutch cocoa powder
- 1.5 cups vegetable oil
- 1 cup buttermilk
- 1 teaspoon vinegar
- 1 teaspoon pure vanilla
- 4 ounces flavorless beet food color

Farnum's Finest Sweet Potato Pie

- 3 cups mashed sweet potato
- 1/2 cup evaporated milk
- 3 tablespoons orange juice
- 4 large eggs
- 1 teaspoon lemon juice
- 2 tablespoons flour
- 3 cups granulated sugar
- 2 teaspoons cinnamon
- 1/4 teaspoon nutmeg
- 2 tablespoons butter

✦✦✦✦✦✦✦ ABOUT ✦✦✦✦✦✦✦
Dr. Samuel Gilmore

Dr. Samuel Gilmore was born and raised in Salisbury, N.C. on December 26, 1934 to Reverend George and Annabelle Gilmore. He was the second youngest of six children. As a child, he would help his father in their garden, where he developed a love and skill for horticulture. He began to work for a woman in town, named Ms. Foster, who grew flowers for local florist shops. Samuel graduated from Price Highschool in Salisbury, N.C. and served in the Air Force from 1954–1958. In the fall of 1958, Samuel left the military and attended Livingston College in North Carolina. After a brief time in school, Samuel returned to the military and was stationed in Texas, Korea, and Arizona before parting after 10 years of service.

Upon leaving the military, Samuel attended and graduated from aeronautics school in Philadelphia and went on to work for Eastern Airlines in New York as an aircraft mechanic. In 1973, Samuel was saved and delivered by Jesus Christ in Brooklyn, N.Y. under the direction of Apostle Johnnie Washington. He then attended and graduated from Macedonia Theological Seminary school with a doctorate degree. Dr. Samuel Gilmore is currently a pastor in a five-fold ministry, Agape Love in Action Ministries, located in South Jamaica, Queens. His mission is to help lay the foundation to God's kingdom by making disciples out of all nations, organizing families, and developing communities all over the word. These communities will run self-sufficiently and serve our Lord, Jesus Christ.

Phone   917-231-7646

Email   agapeloveinactionministries@outlook.com

Facebook   @SamuelGilmore

MY LIFE'S JOURNEY TO TRUTH

by Dr. Samuel Gilmore

As we look around today, we can see that there are many problems among black people that haven't been resolved since the time we have come out of slavery. An example is the dysfunctional family, which has spiraled into many other problems. This dysfunction did not occur by chance but was rather a design to break up the black family in order to control and hinder us from becoming self-sufficient and independent.

There were tactics of failure used in the system of slavery. These tactics included the division of the family by separating mothers and fathers from their children, the hindrance of reading and writing and the deliberate failure to give the land promised to black people. This major tactic of not giving us land would force our ancestors to come back and work for previous slaver masters, which resulted in the sharecropping system.

Slavery was the result of people being disobedient to God and His laws. Anytime we move away from God, we move away from His protection. It is not necessary for us to look backwards to the things that hurt us, except as a lesson to help us move forward. It is now time for us, as black people, to resolve the problems that have been hindering us for over 150 years.

All the things that are going on in the world are simply symptoms of a problem. We cannot continue to deal with the symptom; we must deal with the root of the problem! The world contains international problems, such as war, and national problems, such as disease and hunger. Problems within the cities include homelessness, or community and neighborhood issues such as gang violence and drugs, unemployment, incarceration, and the raising of children in single parent homes. All of these are at an all-time high.

God has given us many strategies to turn us around as a people. First, we must align ourselves with His laws and principals, so that whatever we do will not be contrary to the plans that He has for us.

We have been disobedient to God since the beginning, starting with Adam and Eve. The first commandment given by God to mankind is stated in Genesis 1:27-28 as, *"So God created man in his own image, in the image of God created him; male and female created he them. And God blessed them, and God said unto them, be fruitful and multiply, and replenish the earth, and subdue it: and have dominion over the fish of the sea, and over the fowl of the air, and over every living thing that moveth upon the earth."* In Genesis 27, God is telling us we are made in His image and likeness. We should meditate on this, to realize that we are the pinnacle of all His creations and we are capable of doing anything at its highest level. At the Tower of Babel, we were all one people that spoke one language. God said whatever we imagined we would be able to accomplish.

In Genesis 1:28, God gives man his first commandment by telling him to be fruitful, multiply, and take dominion over the earth. If you look up the definition of dominion, it means sovereignty or control. Sovereignty means to have supreme power or authority. God intended for man to multiply, which would give him help so he could take control and authority through God's supreme power.

God always gives us a pattern of what He wants us to do. When He created Adam and Eve, He put them into a garden. When I was a child, my father told me that God intended for Adam and Eve to plant gardens all over the world. This has guided my understanding of what God's plan for man should be. Everything that Adam and Eve needed, God put into the garden. What an enormous garden this must have been, with four rivers flowing out of it. Reflecting on the problems we are facing today, we should look at the pattern God has given us to strive and fulfill our needs. Taking dominion in the present day would mean building our own self-sufficient communities. This would entail producing and creating every vital thing we would need on our own land.

Imagine black people building our own houses, making our own clothes and furniture, producing our own crops, and, most importantly, having our own school system and curriculum that aligns with God. The world has its way of doing things, but God has His way too. *"Therefore, come out from among them and be separate, says the Lord ..."* (2Corinthians 6:17). We can't depend on this world's education system to teach us how to live like God has intended us to live. How can our children become successful when they have deliberately been left out? Now it's time for us to recognize the hand of God throughout the history of mankind. We must write our own books based on the truth.

I don't feel that we, as black people, have been fully engaged in educating our own people. We have assumed the educational system was all we need. But if we look at other cultural groups, they have always had supplementary educational curriculums available afterschool and still do! This gave them an understanding of the importance of their history and culture. I believe that our churches need to adopt a similar format. We should be opening the doors of the church seven days a week. Five of those days can be used to feed and teach the children after school. During this time period, they can learn about God and their history and all the other things about our culture that have been left out of the school curriculum. We should be working in concert to make sure the children are successful. We should be accountable for one another.

THE ROOT: The home has been broken since slavery, and we must fix it. When we have a breakdown in the family or in the home, there should be something organized and structurally in place in the community, school, and church to make sure the child's needs are taken care of. It is clear that God would never leave a task, especially this great, up to one individual; we have to do this together.

When we were in slavery in Egypt, we were allowed to keep our names, our religion, and our culture. Slavery here in America was different from any other slavery that ever existed, because it stripped us of everything. It was used for evil. God gave us Jesus, and we have Him until this day! Our ancestors prayed for their deliverance out of slavery. They would work all day and pray all night, way back in the woods, in brush harbors, because if they got caught praying, they would be killed. It may have taken 350 years for them to be delivered, but their prayers resulted in freedom. God said, in His word, *"If my people who are called by my name will humble themselves and pray and seek my face, and turn from their wicked ways, then I will hear from heaven, and forgive their sin and heal their land."* (2Chronicles 7:14)

Throughout the Bible, there has been evidence of prayer delivering God's people out of their situations. Not only were they delivered but, in most cases, they received land. In the book of Exodus chapter 3, an angel appeared to Moses in the form of flames of fire within a bush. *"And the Lord said, I have surely seen the affliction of my people which are in Egypt, and have heard their cry because of their slave drivers; for I know their sorrows; And I am come down to deliver them out of the hand of the Egyptians, and bring them up out of that land, unto a land flowing with milk and honey..."* (Exodus 3:7-8) In the book of Daniel, the Prophet realizes the curse God put on his people of 70 years enslavement to Babylon was up, and there was a necessity to pray for their release. He didn't go to the King on the matter or protest with the people, He went on a fast and prayed to God. Through prayer, God softened the heart of King Cyrus, and the king allowed the Israelites to return to Jerusalem to rebuild their temple. In the present day, we are so quick to protest for our rights instead of combining protest with prayer. By protesting and not praying, we're getting worldly results, but not spiritual results. This is spiritual warfare, *"For we wrestle not against flesh and blood, but against principalities, against powers, against the rulers of the darkness of this world, against spiritual wickedness in high places"* (Ephesians 6:12).

The Bible states the Romans killed James with the sword and they put Peter in jail, but then the people prayed without ceasing and Peter was released. We should understand that prayer really does change things. If the people would have prayed without ceasing in the first place, James's fate could have been different. Prayer can change the course of history, and it will change the problems we face today. Prayer changes things, but are we praying? Are we praying collectively? Are we praying on one accord? Or, maybe we haven't been taught the importance of prayer. In the book of Acts chapter 2, when they were all on one accord, the Holy Ghost fell. When you keep praying, God will put us on one accord so we can fully understand what He is saying. Prayer is seeking God's will.

We think we know God's plan, but do we really? The Bible says, *"For as the heavens are higher than the earth, so are my ways higher than your ways, and my thoughts than your thoughts"* (Isaiah 55:9). God's word also says, *"For we know in part, and we prophesy in part"* (1Corinthians 13:9).

If we want a community to thrive, we must pray. We, as Black people, don't have ownership within the jobs that we're occupying or the community we live in. We can't pass down a city, state, or federal job to our children. More importantly, society's strategy is to privatize the workforce to remove the Black people from the jobs we've become so secure in. I believe that we need to create an inheritance for the generations to come. We need to begin to adopt a generational mindset, which will start with the organization of the family. Every family that came out of slavery should have a piece of land. Each piece of land that the family inherits or purchases will become an inheritance for the later generations. I also believe that each black family should put up so much money a month to invest in family insurance. Every month, we pay for several insurance policies on cars, life, medical, retirement, homes, and the list can go on and on. Now, we need a family insurance that will take care of family members that fall through the cracks. Some lose their jobs, some become homeless, some are in and out of prison, etc. These people, according to God's plan, are our responsibility, not the responsibility of the city, state, or federal government. This insurance can also help fund the purchasing and building up of the land to start a community.

It's been 400 years, from 1619–2019, that we have been on the plantation or holding onto a plantation mentality, and now it's time for our exodus. But will we be ready to accept the responsibility of building our own communities so we can become a blessing to the other nations? When Israel left Egypt, God gave them the land of Canaan, which was already built and flowing with milk and honey. It was Israel's responsibility to run the Canaanites out and set up the land for themselves. In our case, we initially built this land as slaves. We were promised land, but we never received it. Through the Atlantic slave trade, a stock market was birthed. Through our oppression of the cotton picking, the stock market thrived. Our ancestors built many cities and communities that were burned or destroyed, such as Wilmington, NC, Durham, NC, Chicago, Los Angeles, Seneca Village in NYC, and Black Wall Street in Greenwood, Tulsa, OK, along with many more.

The people that God used to set this country up didn't follow God's commandment to go into the world and make disciples (Matthew 28:19-20). God made it easy for them, and brought all the nations of the world right here. God set up America as a land of many nations, so that they would become disciples and be blessed. Instead of making disciples, they brought the Africans here and enslaved them. They slaughtered the Indians and took their land. If they would have been obedient to God's word, the Indians would have given them the land in love and the Africans would have helped them build up the land for little or nothing. Now is a good time for America to come together in prayer and humble ourselves, and repent of our sins so that God can forgive us and lift us up so that we can bring peace to the world, through the prince of peace, Jesus Christ.

God said, *"Thy kingdom come, Thy will be done, on earth as it is in heaven..."* (Matthew 6:10). We don't have to wait for Jesus to return. God wants us to set up a paradise now. Since Adam and Eve, we have never really understood how to take dominion over God's creation. Israel had to fight to get land when they came out of Egypt, but America already has land that we can use to take dominion. God always blesses us through the land. Once we get a piece of land, we will let Jesus become the Lord of the land and be obedient to His commandments. *"Thou shalt love thy God with all thy heart, and all thy soul, and all thy mind."* This is the first and great commandment. And the second is *"like unto it, thou shalt love thy neighbor as thyself. On these two commandments hang all the law and the prophets"* (Matthew 22:37-40).

This land will be used to build a community, which will begin the building of God's kingdom. We will make disciples out of all the nations of people who want to be a part of the community. The first community built will be a model of how to set up other communities in other cities and states. Eventually, all the different nations of people will be able to purchase land in their own countries and set up these communities for their people. Remember: we must be accountable for one another. This is how we as God's people can take dominion and build up God's kingdom all over the world.

All the nations of the world have made mistakes in the past, which caused their downfall. These nations of people are now here in America, looking for us to show them how to be great. They have come here looking for opportunities, because they realize something was missing where they came from. But have we forgotten how to become a great nation? I recently came across a YouTube video from Morning Star Ministries, where a man named Rick Joyner discussed a prophetic vision of a Revolutionary/Civil War approaching in these end times. He stated that God never intended for America to run the British out, but to set up this nation so that it would be liberty and justice for all. He then mentioned that all the nations that came here weren't granted that freedom. If the Europeans that set the country up would have been truly following God's word, there wouldn't have been a Civil War or a Civil Rights movement. The point being: if we don't straighten up as a nation and begin following God and praying, there can be a Revolutionary/Civil war brewing in our near future, considering the state this country is in.

Many events have happened throughout American history to help us realize God's hand in this nation. After the so-called freedom of our ancestors from slavery, they became sharecroppers. The plantation owners never truly wanted them free nor did they want to tend to their own crops, considering the hard work it entailed. They surely didn't want our ancestors to be able to have a portion of their land, but they did want the portion of the crop that would be produced. A failure tactic was surely used to keep our ancestors indebted to them, by constantly adding a tab to their yearly earnings. During the winter months, there was no work on the farm but the farmers needed certain essentials to survive. The landowners had company stores that stocked products that the farmers would need. A tab was created and continuously added money unto their debt. When the farmer's crop was finally produced, it never covered the bill that our ancestors ran up during the winter months. They would eventually have to work another year and never made enough from their crop to become independent. This vicious cycle continued until God intervened and sent the boll weevil, a beetle that feeds on cotton buds, to eat all the cotton crop throughout the South. This devastated the entire cotton industry and forced the landowners to let the sharecroppers go, resulting in the great migration from the south.

During the 1930s, God sent a bumper crop to the U.S. The bumper crop, meaning unusually large, resulted in an abundance of food harvested for the American agriculture industry. The food would be stored in warehouses in the Midwest, but when the abundance was too great, they would load the food onto ships and dump it into the ocean on the west coast. My father once told me because of this great sin, God sent a windstorm called a dust bowl, which took six inches of the top soil and blew it into the ocean. This once again devastated the agricultural industry. In 1906, the same time as the great revival in California under the leadership of William Seymour, an earthquake erupted in San Francisco. A devastating fire broke out and lasted for several days, resulting in the destruction of 80% of the city and a death toll of 3,000 people. A prophet was sent to the city to tell the people that the earthquake was sent from God. God tried to make us understand through these incidents that we must follow Him.

As you come to the conclusion of this chapter, it might be a good idea to look over the history of mankind, so we can see why there were so many problems. As stated previously, all our problems are just symptoms of a root problem: that we are not following God. The wonderful thing about God is, He gives us mercy and so many chances. Those who really believe that Jesus is the Messiah have a chance to implement God's end time plan of taking dominion by building communities and making disciples of all the nations. At the Tower of Babel, the word of God says, we were all one people that spoke one language, but the people began to build monuments for themselves instead of taking dominion over God's creation. Therefore, God had to come down and change their language, which was a curse so they couldn't understand each other and work together.

Now, He sent Jesus to bring us all into one people through His blood, and we can do the things God wants us to do. We can build communities all across America and make disciples out of all the people from all around the world.

We can help them build communities in their countries and make disciples of their people. In doing so, we will be able to establish the kingdom of God, because we know that Satan has had a free run since the beginning. It's now time for the children of God to do His will, *"For [even the whole] creation [all nature] waits eagerly for the children of God to be revealed. For the creation was subjected to frustration, not by the will of the one who subjected it, in hope that the creation itself will be liberated from its bondage to decay and brought into the freedom and glory of the children of God"* (Romans 8:19-21). Furthermore, at this time, we must all forgive each other, because we all make mistakes and Jesus said at the cross, *"Forgive them for they know not what they do."* The Bible also states, *"when the righteous rule, there is peace in the land"*, so, if we really want peace, we must follow the prince of peace, Jesus Christ our Lord, thereby bringing peace throughout the entire world.

FINAL WORDS

We hope that you were empowered by the stories we have shared with you. We believe that they have the ability to change your life. We are sure that, while reading some of them, you probably thought about your own story. Let's face it: we've all experienced a setback that positioned us for a comeback. This book is one of the first of the *Our Stories, Our Voices: Black Men Speak Their Truth* anthology series. If you would like to participate with us on future projects, please contact us at collaborativeexperience@gmail.com

You might also be interested in your own single-title book project or book anthology project for you and your tribe and would like us to assist you. If so, please contact us. We can help you. Contact us so we can discuss how we can assist you in making your author dreams come true. You can reach either Toni or Julia by emailing collaborativeexperience@gmail.com or calling us at 646-421-0830 or 917-501-6780. You can also visit us online at www.thecollaborativeexperience.com